T0390748

Dancing in Time

ROBERT HYLTON

Dancing in Time

THE HISTORY OF MOVING AND SHAKING

First published in 2022 by
The British Library
96 Euston Road
London NW1 2DB

ISBN 978 0 7123 5461 5

British Library Cataloguing in Publication Data
A catalogue record for this publication is available from the British Library

Picture Research by Sally Nicholls
Designed by Steve Russell / aka-designaholic.com
Printed and bound in the Czech Republic by Finidr

MIX
Paper from
responsible sources
FSC
www.fsc.org
FSC® C014138

CONTENTS

FOREWORD

DANCING IS SO much more than physical exercise. It's self-expression, giving us permission to take up space and be our true selves. It's entertainment, filling ballrooms and arenas with audiences eager to see breathtaking leaps, lifts and spins. Whether you're dancing solo or with a partner, it's a way to connect and communicate – with friends, family or complete strangers.

But dance can even go a step further. It has the power to connect us to the past. When I dance, I celebrate all the dancers who have come before me, their genius as well as their struggles. It's so important to know how we got here, and why so many millions of people around the global love dance as much as they do. Dance encourages us to embrace other cultures, but it can also be an empowering way to connect with our own roots.

While working on *Strictly Come Dancing*, I could immediately see the transformative power of dance on people who'd never tried it before. They lit up with the beauty of the waltz, the sensuality of the tango, the freedom of jive and the pure joy of samba. You can see the same joy on the pages of *Dancing in Time*. These pages are not just full of history – they are full of life. They celebrate legendary dancers like the performer Josephine Baker, the Castle walk creators Vernon and Irene Castle, and the hugely successful 1970s dance group The Lockers.

But it's the forgotten innovators that take centre stage, the unnamed dancers whose rhythms and steps became worldwide phenomena. In reading this book, I am reminded of how important it is to recognise the people throughout history who have made every professional dancer's experience possible, and to pay tribute to those who paved the way. It's a privilege to be a part of this history.

OTI MABUSE

PREFACE

AS WE APPROACH the mid-twenty-first century social-media-based dance has never been so widely available. We are able to view a myriad of dances on screen. As screen-based dance becomes more visible in our everyday, I often question whether we really see the dance embedded in the screen. I can scroll through dance-related visuals on social media for five minutes and not really see any particular dance, as the handheld black mirror blurs from figure to figure. I tend to use YouTube in a more specific way for research purposes. When it comes to the flick and scroll, I veer towards the occasional pause rather than actually watching. Even though dance is a big part of my life – and maybe it's age (I was born in the 1970s and, for reference when reading this book, am a mixed-raced, light-skinned male) – viral dance content on such a scale and with non-stop output is not necessarily made for me, born as I was when social media and handheld devices were only to be found in sci-fi.

That said, the level of dancing on screen at present is incredible; it just feels a little overwhelming. Or maybe the speed of social media itself is becoming more challenging than humans can deal with. Books ask for a different attention, holding not scrolling, although there is occasional flicking. My attention to social media may change in time. I may go through a peak or low of connecting to screen-based dance. I like to keep up with dance trends so it can be difficult to stay away from the screen completely. The availability of information in different forms is a welcome inclusion in an ever-expanding cultural and creative space. Whichever way you experience dance moments of stillness are precious; whether as mover or watcher it is the shared moments, the memories and the love of dance that I draw on in this book.

And I'll leave you with this thought: dance like no one is watching.

OPPOSITE Ballroom dancers, print by
Henri Fournier, 1914.

INTRODUCTION

WHILE RESEARCHING and writing *Dancing in Time* I often asked myself: what am I looking for? Is this a history of the visual imagery of dance or is it about context: the who, the why, the where? The potential for pictorial analyses was always lingering, but the more I pondered on the 'what', the more I realised that *Dancing in Time* is about people. Dance is reflected through human stories from many different places with complex histories, rhythms and meanings. Simply put it is about how generations of people have danced in diverse ways and for different reasons.

I have always danced, whether consciously or not. My mum often tells a story from when I was about 5 years old, in the mid-1970s. As many families did then we were at the cinema watching a Saturday morning film (we think *Chitty Chitty Bang Bang*). I must admit I have no memory of my spontaneous outburst, but I suddenly got up and started dancing in the aisle, much to the amusement and dismay of my family and other audience members. So it seems I was born to dance. Since that morning in the cinema my relationship with dance has evolved, drawing me to hip hop dance styles, then moving me towards contemporary dance and classical ballet. Dance has imprinted itself onto my core through work, rest and play, both professionally and personally. This of course is not a unique experience; well, maybe the 5-year-old dancing in the cinema aisle is.

Dance in any shape or form is a story of human expression and shared experience; millions of people over centuries and around the world have moved their bodies and danced, some instinctively, some in a formal way and some even reluctantly. This book brings together some of the most wonderful images that capture lived experience and dancing bodies, images that carry a multitude of energies and reflect the spirit, personalities and mysteries of those dancers, held in a moment in time by a photographic lens or illustration. They present a tangible, changing narrative of human experience, expressed through pictorial stories of class, power, race, gender, sexual liberation and so much more. Whether the minuet, waltz, Charleston or twist, dance has always been intertwined with what is happening in the world.

What drives me most as I shift my role from dancer to writer to reader is the experience of looking and imagining. *Dancing in Time* provides a collection of moments when, in your imagination, you can place yourself

OPPOSITE Front cover to piano score for 'Stella', a polka by Emile Ettling, 1850. Extract from the ballet *Stella ou les Contrebandiers* by Arthur Saint-Léon, music by Cesare Pugni.

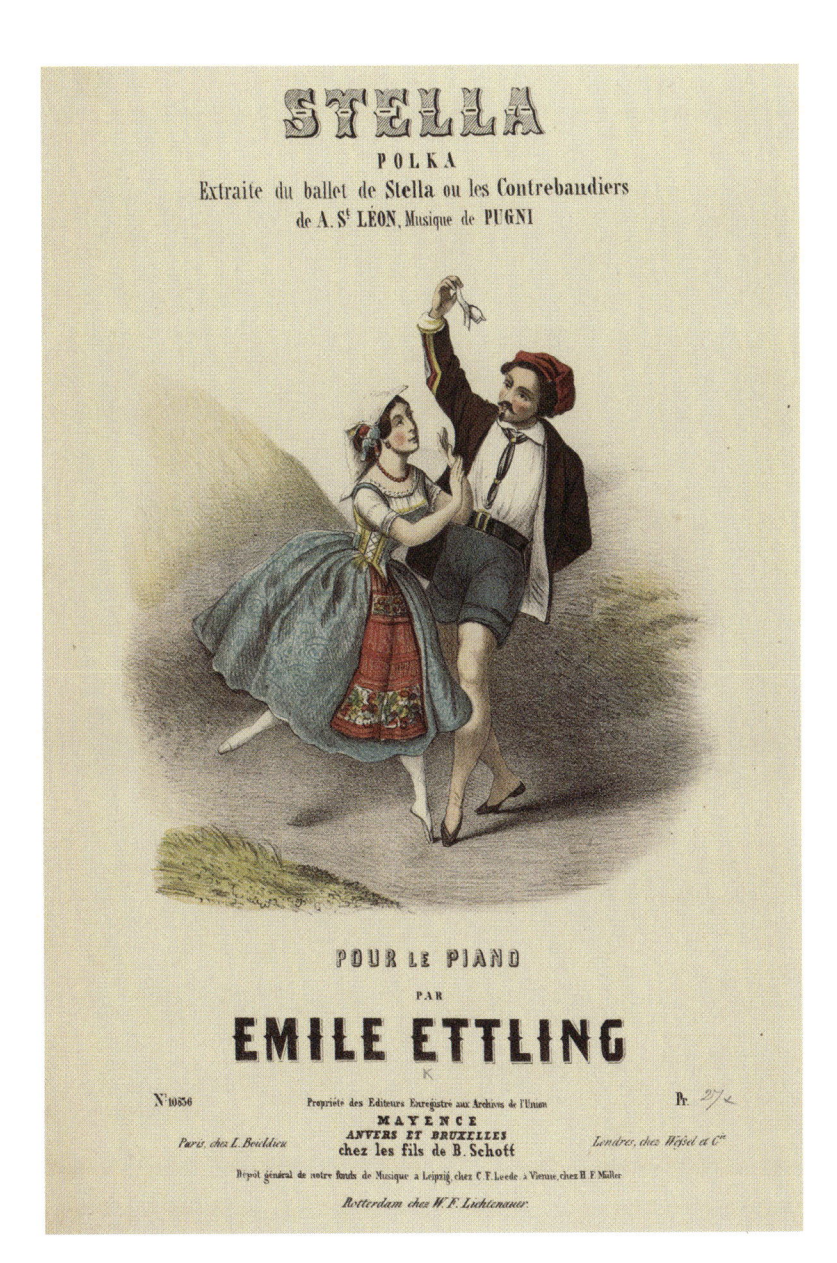

alongside the subjects in the images, as you move from page to page. It's about that thing that humans do, that thing called dancing: expressing ourselves through our bodies away from the everyday. It's about escaping.

There are of course also challenges when looking at images from times when displays of class, properness, politics, gender, pleasure, nationalism, affluence, patriarchy, sexuality and so on seem far removed from who we are today. Dances such as the tango, waltz or Charleston, which were once seen as endangering our youth, are now welcomed into our popular culture. In a similar way social media and music videos are the new space for potentially dangerous dancing and the new measure of what is or is not considered proper in an ever-changing dancing world.

Writing *Dancing in Time* has enhanced my own understanding, and more so my appreciation, of different dance forms. I have even grown to like the stuffiness and formality of some of the dances of old that are far removed from my hip hop self. Dance is a lens through which we can explore different places and people and better understand them.

By momentarily placing yourself within the images, as you might when watching a costume drama, you can involve yourself not just in the viewing, but in the visualising of a different body or era. Dance at its best, whether experienced as performer,

partygoer or casual two-stepper, is about losing yourself. Who knows? While reading this book you may be inspired to have a gentle sway or nod to a favourite musical choice, even to create a dance of your own, adding your story to the history of dance.

Strictly Come Dancing in the UK and *Dancing with the Stars* in the US do an excellent job of introducing different dance forms to the masses. That said, they are televised entertainment shows, not documentaries, and it's the dance studios and classrooms that bear the brunt of educational responsibility. As a dance educator it is difficult not to present the history of dance when teaching movement or choreography. Social experience and history are intertwined within dance. I think how much you understand about both the history and movement of the dance you wish to learn shows in your body.

When teaching I often make the analogy that football fans tend to know everything about every football team – the wins, the losses and the history of the players, sometimes over decades. My question to the students is: shouldn't dance be the same? Becoming a walking dance encyclopaedia will take a long time, so it's more about inspiring a will and enthusiasm in young dancers to understand that learning dance is not only a physical experience, but also a psychological one.

OPPOSITE Sheet music for 'Ladies of the Dance' by Richard A. Whiting, c.1929. Featured in the film *The Dance of Life*.

CHAPTER 01.

EUROPEAN MELODIES

IT'S HARD TO believe that dances such as the waltz were once seen as endangering the young, as uncivilised practices that would dismantle the core of nineteenth-century living. The Pope and many other guardians of moral values sought to ban the waltz on the grounds that it would degrade society. Later, in the early twentieth century, ragtime music and animal dances such as the turkey trot became a familiar feature in our dancing spaces, and the tango and its erotic gestures pushed the boundaries of dancing acceptability. These dances, like the waltz, introduced the potential to corrupt the youth through contact dancing and close proximity between the sexes, providing opportunities for touch and intimacy not found in dances of old such as the minuet, quadrille or cotillion. Strict structures of good etiquette and properness were considered of the utmost importance to the way one should live and dance.

Epitomising these values was the minuet, an elegant partner dance that dominated aristocratic ballrooms in Europe, especially in France and England, from the mid-seventeenth century to the mid-eighteenth century, and is thought to have developed from a French folk dance, the *branle de Poitou*. The court version saw dancers,

in order of their social position, demonstrate small, well-placed steps in a slow-paced tempo which allowed for carefully placed bows or curtsies towards their partner through floor patterns such as a figure of eight or, later, a Z pattern. The minuet was especially popular at the court of Louis XIV of France.

The quadrille, meanwhile, had its roots in English country dance. The English dancing master John Playford first put the quadrille on record in 1651 in his series of books *The English Dancing Master: or, plaine and easie rules for the dancing of country dances, with the tune to each dance.*[1] The quadrille in its earliest form was a line dance of alternating men and women with four couples facing each other in a square formation; it slowly became a familiar social dance throughout England, then in Europe. Its growing dance-floor success saw the quadrille become one of the most fashionable dances throughout the eighteenth and nineteenth centuries. Dances like the quadrille were passed backwards and forwards between the British Isles, France, Europe and throughout the colonies. They were first known as country dances in England, then *contredanses* in France, and they were eventually reframed in England as 'contra dance'.[2]

OPPOSITE 'The Regular Order of the Minuet', from *The Art of Dancing Explained by Reading and Figures* by Kellom Tomlinson, 1735.

The under written Music is to the Steps contained in this Plate
on their Repetition a Second Time between the Plates XI and XII.

To the R.t Hon:ble Brownlow Lord Burleigh Son to the Earl of Exeter, and the R.t Hon:ble the Lady Margaret Sophia Cecil his Sister, this Plate is most humbly Inscribed by their Hon.rs most oblig'd Servant ———— Kellom Tomlinson.

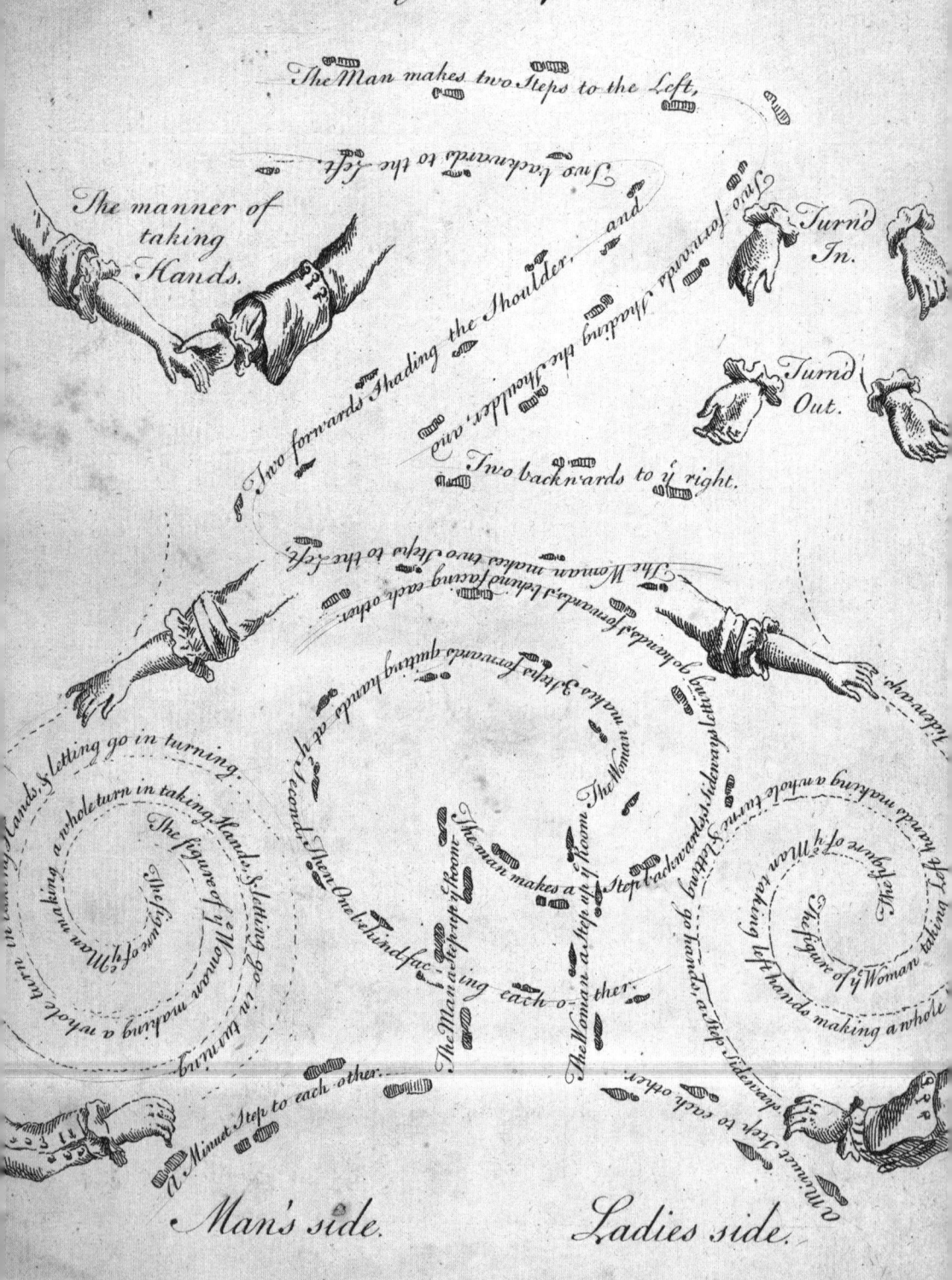

The compleat Figure of the Minuet.

In France the quadrille developed further through more intricate floor patterns and intertwining bodies passing and crossing each other. The umbrella term quadrille comprised four or five *contredanses* such as the *tour de deux mains* (two-hand dance), in which couples held hands and turned, and the *chaîne des dames* (ladies' chain), in which opposite women first passed each other by the right hand, then each gave her left hand to the opposite man. The man then turned her to his side to re-set the position and formation of the group.

The cotillion was also an eighteenth- and nineteenth-century French court dance and arrived in France as a precursor to the quadrille. Lively and energetic, it too was danced by four couples in a square set facing inwards; opposing couples alternated geometric patterns. During the nineteenth century cotillion floor patterns became more varied and the dancing was combined with the giving of presents. In dances such as these, properness and etiquette were an important part of maintaining the social structure of the elite and were passed from generation to generation. Coded social behaviours became inextricably linked with dance events.

These early court dances originated from peasant dances that were curated and refined to become either the ballroom dancing we now know or the beginnings of classical ballet. Court dancing and dances such as the quadrille were set by the dancing masters and carefully detailed in dancing manuals to ensure uniformity in the ballroom.[3] Those who developed dance and the proper ways of social etiquette for the elite, or even royalty such as Queen Victoria,[4] were seen as important members of society. The dancing masters' manuals or written instructional dance sheets, to which the working classes did not have access, provided a way to separate people by social status and dance became a tool to determine who could wield social and economic power.

The dancing masters were the authorities, often developing and choreographing what was to be danced in the royal courts or for the social elite in the nineteenth century and before. The development of dance was inherently collaborative; as people migrated to find work, or landowners came from the city to visit their various country estates, they brought dance with them. This mixing of classes was an opportunity for the elite to observe or join in with working-class dances, which they then reframed and

OPPOSITE 'The Compleat Figure of the Minuet', from *An Easy Introduction to Dancing: or, The Movements in the Minuet Fully Explained* by George Bickham, c.1755.

ABOVE (top) Titlepage from *The English Dancing Master: or, plain and easie rules for the dancing of country dances, with the tune to each dance* by John Playford, 1651. (bottom) Titlepage from *Le Maître à Danser, or the Art of Dancing Quadrilles … by a Celebrated French Performer and Teacher...*, 1818.

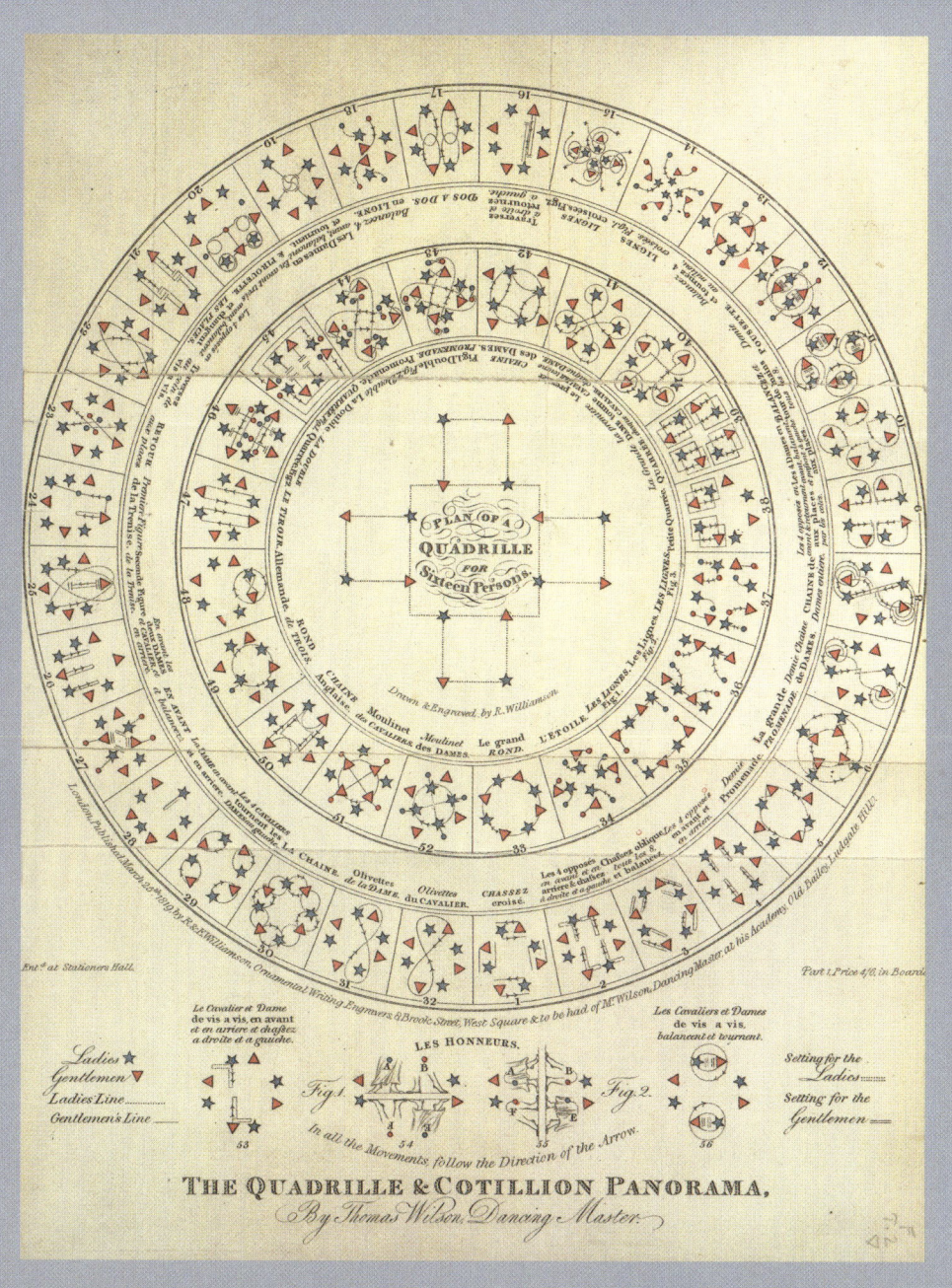

ABOVE *The Quadrille & Cotillion Panorama. A Treatise on Quadrille Dancing, in Two Parts, etc.* by Thomas Wilson (Dancing Master), 1818.

FOLLOWING PAGES 'The First Quadrille at Almack's', illustration from *The Reminiscences and Recollections of Captain Gronow ... 1810–1860* by Rees Howell Gronow, 1892.

MARQUIS OF WORCESTER.

LADY JERSEY.

THE FIRST Q

CLANRONALD MACDONALD. LADY WORCESTER.

AT ALMACK'S.

THE FIVE POSITIONS OF DANCING.

The Figures shew the positions of the Learner,
and the Feet that of a finish'd Dancer.

made exclusive. Sometimes the dancing masters had free rein in devising the new dances, at other times they worked alongside their employers, facilitating the tastes of royalty or the members of the elite to whose households they belonged by dictating European dance-floor tastes.

The waltz, born out of Vienna and Austria as early as the seventeenth century, was a turning, gliding dance but, most importantly, a dance with a close hold that gained a reputation for being obscene. Though it was said to be a dance for prostitutes and mistresses it spread across Europe and around the world. Earlier dances were threatened by the simplicity of the waltz. The complexity of cotillions or the minuet that relied on dancing masters and daily practice became less attractive. Keeping up to date with the detail and latest variations of such dances in order to maintain one's status was cast aside for the ease of the waltz. Along with that the waltz could potentially put the dancing masters out of a job as it required less professional tuition.

The opportunity for body-to-body contact in the holding and close proximity of the waltz must have been a revelation to those used to the well-known steps and arrangements of country dances,[5] as English folk dance became ordered and fashionable in royal courts and for the elite. One thing life teaches is that if the young are told not to do something, they will run straight to it – rock 'n' roll, the twist, you name it – and it seems the waltz was an early example of this youthful rebellion.

The ballrooms of the time were also carefully chaperoned events that would ensure a young lady's reputation was kept in high order, but there were ways in which conversation and flirtatious gestures could be covertly sent across the room. Women's fans, both fashion accessories and a convenient way to cool down in between dances, helped to develop the art of flirtatious behaviour in the ballroom, adding extra layers to the coded structures of the dance floor.[6]

The use of a fan was often a method of signalling one's intention and indicating an interest (or not) in dancing with a partner. For example if a lady were to fan herself slowly it would mean she was engaged or unavailable. If she were to fan at a faster pace, however, it would mean she was unattached and independent. If she were to shut her fan it would mean there was no chance of any kind of engagement. More positive an action for a potential suitor

OPPOSITE 'The Five Positions of Dancing', from *An Analysis of Country Dancing: Wherein Are Displayed All the Figures Ever Used in Country Dances, etc.* by Thomas Wilson (Dancing Master), 1808.

FOLLOWING PAGES Frontispiece plate to *A Description of the Correct Method of Waltzing...* by Thomas Wilson (Dancing Master), 1816.

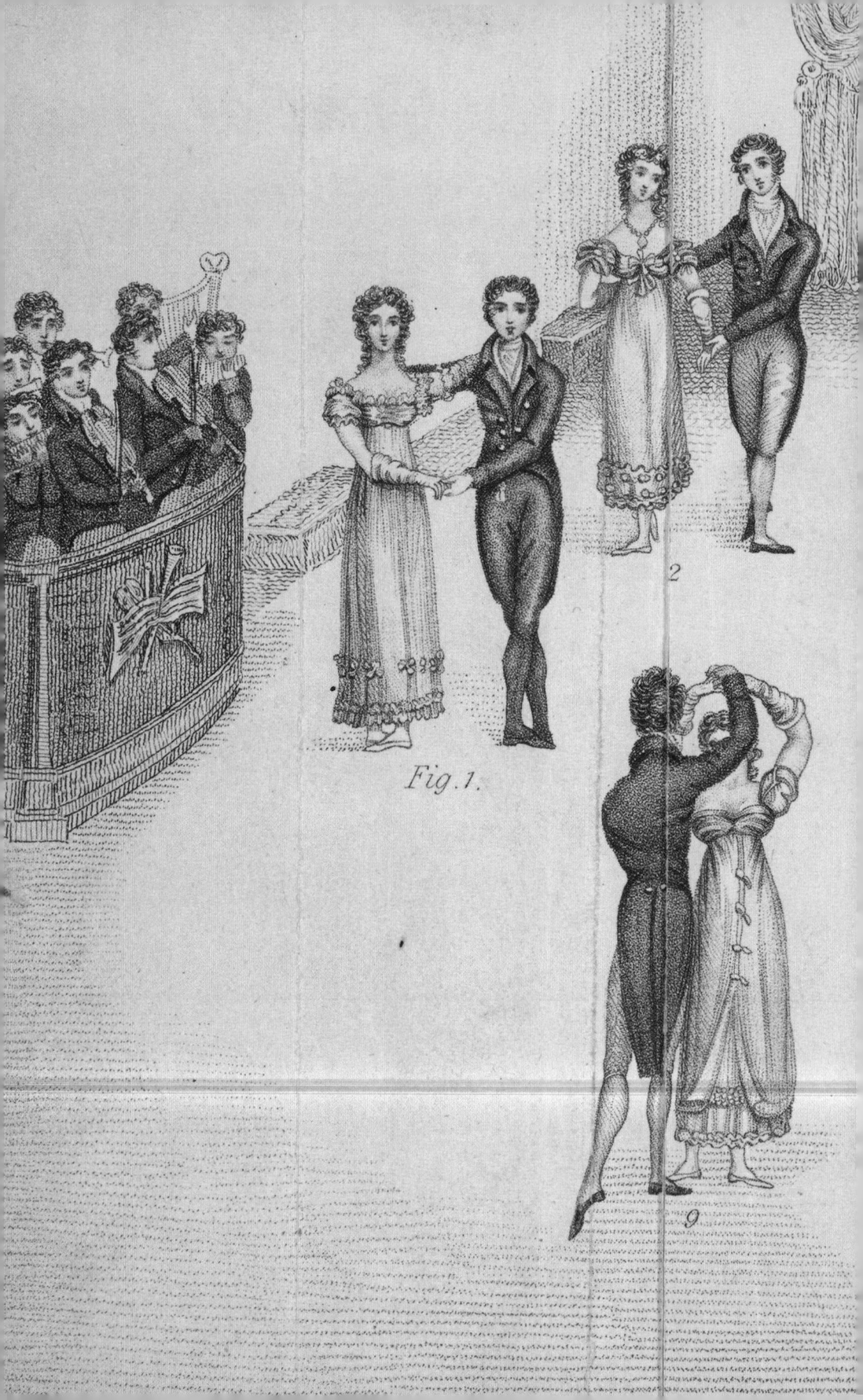

Fig.1.

2

9

would be the deliberate and repetitive opening and shutting of her fan, which meant she was interested. Spending one's night reading or gesturing your love interests, along with remembering all the dance steps, made ballroom dancing a very complex business – a living theatre of sub-plots, dance steps and ballroom bravado.

The popularity of the waltz grew and grew. From the early eighteenth century it spread to the United States and by the mid-nineteenth century it was an established favourite in European and American ballrooms. The spread of the waltz was helped by the music of two Austrian composers, Joseph Lanner (1801-1843) and Johann Strauss I (1804-1849), who heightened the excitement and pace on the dance floor by setting a new standard of musical accompaniment to the waltz through the Viennese waltz, a faster version. The choice of slow waltzes and fast waltzes added variation, pace and the opportunity for enthusiastic dancers to express themselves in different ways.

The excitement of the dancers who waltzed their nights away is understandable. Even Queen Victoria, who was a keen and very capable ballroom dancer, was said to have a great fondness for the waltz (also the polka)

although it is said that she initially took against the waltz due to its perceived lack of civility, and it was originally thought to be improper for the royal court.[7] This dance, once perceived as vulgar like many other dances, was to slowly evolve into refined sophistication. In fact witnessed today it may even look too refined to modern eyes as time has softened what was once seen as dangerous.

There were several other dances such as the mazurka or polka that brought life to many a dance floor and ballroom. Based in Polish folk music and dance tradition, the mazurka is thought to have originated in the sixteenth century, arriving and establishing itself in Europe in the mid-nineteenth century. A lively dance with four to eight couples, it involved stamping feet, clicking heels, held hands and turning and weaving in, which also allowed for improvisation.

The polka was originally a Czech folk dance and genre of music, thought to have originated in Bohemia. Like the mazurka, it gained popularity throughout Europe in the mid-nineteenth century. Dancers chose and developed for themselves how they danced polka, as couples or in groups, alongside pre-set formation dances. The polka is characterised by three quick steps and

OPPOSITE (top) 'La Walse' by James Gillray, from *Le Bon Genre*, 1810. (bottom) Johann Strauss II, 'An der schönen blauen Donau', from *Dr. Otto Böhler's Schattenbilder*, 1914.

a hop in a circular motion over as much space as the room will allow; skipping, hopping, close holds, holding hands and letting go combine to create a dance of great energy, pace and playful floor patterns, including dancers weaving in and out of each other with near misses.

These folk dances were absorbed into classical ballet, initially an Italian dance form, then transformed from social to professional through the Académie Royale de Danse,[8] established by Louis XIV in Paris in 1661 and the first dance institution founded in the Western world. It was a symbol that displayed status and demonstrated cultural and economic power, cultivating nationalism and cultural dominance for France as the European elite. This development refocused the nineteenth-century European narrative on national identity and hierarchical histories that held ambitions of political power. Dance functioned as an oppressive structure and a resource for propaganda, but it was also a means for plain old fun.

Quadrille, country dance, *contredanse*, grand march, waltz, polka, mazurka, schottische, cotillion, galop and minuet, along with jig, clog and reel – rhythmic dances that focus on the feet and leg patterns – as well as many others, were danced not just in Europe but,

as we will see later, exported to the New World, where there was a meeting of African and European dance steps that led to a cross-pollination and eventually morphed into tap, tango and many other dances we know today.

One event on record in the late eighteenth century gives context to London society and particularly Black dance culture in Britain at the time. The *London Chronicle* reported on 17 February 1764 that 57 Black people attended a party in a public house in Fleet Street, London – a mix of men and women who were drinking and dancing. The music was played by violins and other instruments. No whites were allowed to be present.[9] The quadrille was a popular dance in the Caribbean, so there is no doubt that the dancing would have been heavily laden with European formality juxtaposed with African rhythm. I imagine it would have been a great party and it certainly challenges our understanding of Georgian life and dancing in this period.

In the mid-nineteenth century the grand march was the first dance of the evening in the ballrooms of the elite. Led by the master of ceremonies, it was a formal introduction to the event, for attendees to familiarise themselves with who was in the ballroom. Men and women lined up opposite each

OPPOSITE Lithographic music cover to eight pages of *Queen Victoria's Dances. As Danced by Her Majesty Queen Victoria and Prince Albert*, c.1848. The lithograph by Thomas S. Wagner & James McGuigan shows Queen Victoria and Prince Albert in open social position.

32

OPPOSITE Score for 'National Polish Wedding', a mazurka by Valentine Dobrowolski, 1862.

THIS PAGE (top left) 'La Polkamanie: La Leçon chez Cellarius', hand-coloured lithograph by Charles Vernier, c.1840-9. (top right) 'La Polka', originally published as plate 64 of the Victor Dollet series, *Galerie dramatique, costumes des théâtres de Paris, tome 1*, 1840s. (bottom) 'Lowest "Life in London": Tom, Jerry and Logic among the unsophisticated Sons and Daughters of Nature at "All Max" in the East, 1821. From *Life in London* by Pierce Egan, 1823.

other and the man then offered his right arm to his partner, who rested her fingertips at the crook of his arm. Then the dancers promenaded around the outside of the room, marching in step to the time of the music, in all their finery. The dancers were placed in order of rank if it was a military affair, or according to their social position; this displayed the play of hierarchy throughout the grand march. The grand march varied in how long the promenading lasted, depending on the number of attendees, as there was a potential, if there were many, for the slow pace of the promenade to become tedious.

Another popular ballroom dance at that time was the schottische, a partner dance thought to have come from Bohemia. Its basic format is two side steps to the left and right, then a turn in four steps. The galop, thought to be of Hungarian origin, also arrived in France and England in the nineteenth century: a simple but lively partner dance that focused on the *chassé* movement – sliding forward – and was danced around the ballroom.

If I were to imagine myself waltzing or dancing the energised patterns of the polka, be it in the surroundings of a royal court, a private ballroom of the elite or a village square of the workers, I would be inhabiting the drama and glamour alongside the physical confidence and style of those who danced.

As I usher myself towards that fantasy and try to adopt the style and finesse of these dancing bodies into my own, I can begin a part transformation, a characterisation of another physical self, as an actor might do. Although I am looking at images of long-gone dancers, I get a sense of my body changing. Dance can project your soul and at the same time be a conduit that enables a different identity; a chameleon's tool kit that can change how people see you.

In dance, style is everything. Your posture, clothes and the way you stand or sit are carefully structured gestures that project your place and ambitions. In the courts of Europe and Britain those who were fortunate to dance with the elite all understood that their physicality, gestures and knowledge of etiquette were vital to their position in life. When, where and with whom you danced signalled who you were or aimed to be.

In early ballet those performances sponsored by the wife of Henry IV of France, Marie de' Medici, stand out. Only those with a position in society, such as royalty and diplomats, were invited to attend or perform and the performances were very much a display of power, dynasty and opulence. These early ballets would surely eclipse the glamour of the most ostentatious parties of today. There were lavish costumes

OPPOSITE Score for 'The Kettle-Drum Schottische' by Charles Godfrey, 1866.

THE

KETTLE-DRUM

Schottische.

by

C. Godfrey

SOLO 4/=
DUET 4/=
CORNET OBBLIGATO 6"
SEPTET 3/6
ORCHESTRA 5/=

CRAMER & C° (LIMITED) 201, REGENT STREET.

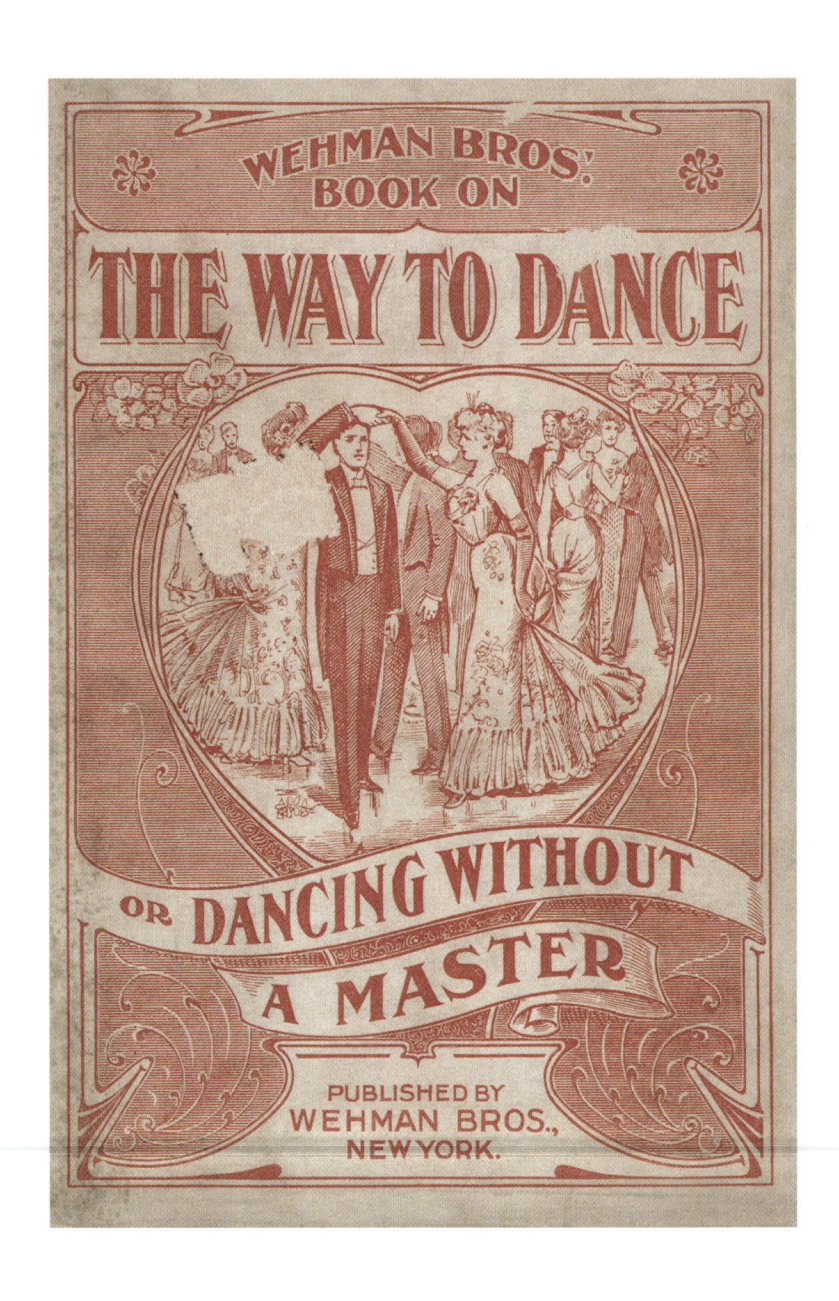

WEHMAN BROS.'
BOOK ON

THE WAY TO DANCE

OR DANCING WITHOUT A MASTER

PUBLISHED BY
WEHMAN BROS.,
NEW YORK.

and jewellery, elaborate theatrical sets and 'novelties' such as dancing dwarfs. Of one of Marie de' Medici's ballets, it is said that the nymphs were wearing such large quantities of diamonds they almost blinded the audience.[10] At first it seems quite bizarre that such opulence and posturing were seen as credible, but today's social and mainstream media follow the same pattern with displays of excess and drama; marketing, PR and spin are nothing new.

There are of course many dancing stories and on the other side were the poor and the peasants who were also living, dancing bodies creating their own meaning, place and entertainment. Dances such as country dances or *contredanses* first developed as social dances of the workers. The surroundings may have been humble but no doubt the dances were full of vigour, representing as they did a temporary pleasure, away from the rigours of manual labour and the harsh realities of day-to-day life, that ignited households and communities with the spirit of dance. They demonstrate that the essence of dance needs neither money nor fancy lights – it is for everyone.

Throughout this book we see two things: the organic development of dance as it spreads from place to place and the need for self-expression. Throughout history people have passed on the dance, music, food and social traditions of their area to others as a form of natural communication and the desire to relate to others through the enjoyment dance can bring. But brutality, conflict and colonialism, and the responses to them, are equally responsible for the shaping of dance culture, as we shall see when European melodies meet African rhythms in the next chapter.

OPPOSITE Front cover to *Wehman Bros.' Book on the Way to Dance, or, Dancing Without a Master*, c.1900.

THIS PAGE Front cover to *How to Dance: A complete ball-room and party guide. Containing all the latest figures, together with old-fashioned and contra dances now in general use...*, 1878.

CHAPTER 02.

AMERICAN RHYTHMS, AFRICAN BEATS

AS EUROPE FOUGHT over, exchanged, lost and won new territories in the nineteenth century and beyond, slavery – the buying and selling of African people – came to darken world history. Although slavery has existed in different times and places in the world, the industrialisation of slavery in this period was to leave fragments of past cultures that would develop and influence modern times, presenting reinvented or misunderstood African memory as American rhythm. By the latter part of the nineteenth century Black people no longer enslaved in the Americas or the Caribbean were now left to find themselves: free but abandoned people having to work out who they were in places they now called home.

In the late 1700s refugees of the French Revolution (the French elite) found themselves in the Americas and specifically New Orleans. English country dances, Irish jigs and Scottish reels were refreshed by the up-to-date minuets and *contredanses* of the French and the ballrooms were reinvigorated – much to the amusement of the African slaves, who, as they watched, mimicked the rigid gesturing bodies and pomp of the Europeans.[11] The music and dance discussed in Chapter 1, now popular in America,

brought a new phase of cross-pollination between European and African cultures, and African dance became Americanised. Free and enslaved Black people gathered in Congo Square in New Orleans to sing and dance, and this triggered the beginnings of jazz.[12]

Dances from the British Isles brought over to the United States by newly arriving immigrants or sailors, such as the jig, clog and reel, with their focus on footwork and rhythm, intertwined themselves with African dance through the mixing of footwork and rhythms that helped develop and influence what became tap dance.[13] In this way buck dancing,[14] a rhythmic stomping of the feet danced by slaves, which carried fragments of African dance, became a precursor to tap. The slaves' mimicry of the European dance and its steps and gestures, such as in the grand march, found its way into the cakewalk, a dance originally known as 'chalk the line',[15] and European melodies and structures were also incorporated into African rhythm to develop ragtime.

Another dance, the jig – a rapid rhythmic footwork dance with rigid torso – was practised in both England and Scotland in

OPPOSITE 'Negro Dance' by Richard Bridgens (artist) and Day & Haghe (lithographer), between 1838 and 1845. Print shows African Trinidadians playing music and dancing.

FOLLOWING PAGES 'Negro Figuranti', from *West India Scenery ... from sketches taken during a voyage to, and residence of seven years in, the island of Trinidad* by Richard Bridgens, 1836.

the sixteenth and seventeenth centuries and in Ireland from the eighteenth century. Clog dancing, a step dance with an emphasis on rhythm from the feet of dancers wearing wooden-soled clogs, is thought to have been developed in the north of England and in Wales and demonstrates many variations. There was also Irish clogging – tap-like in steps but with a louder emphasis to its rhythms. The reel, of Scottish origin and danced in soft shoes, focused on travelling steps and dancing on the spot – flicks of the legs, hops and skips – and is thought to go back as far as the sixteenth century.

Pattin' juba, also known as the hambone, is an African American dance that came out of slavery. It involved stomping the feet as well as slapping and 'patting' the legs, arms and torso to make rhythmic sounds that accompanied improvised solo or dance

challenges.[16] It is thought to have arrived in the United States via the West Indies with origins in Kongo (a Central African kingdom that lay in what is now part of Angola, Democratic Republic of the Congo, Republic of the Congo and southern Gabon). In today's terms we can see variations of pattin' juba, now known as body percussion, on stage through international performance groups such as STOMP – a stylised theatrical performance group that began in Brighton, England, in 1991 and uses the body, objects, acrobatics and pantomime to develop a show based on body rhythm.

Slavery officially ended in the United States in 1865 and, with Jim Crow laws and segregation ready to take its place, many freed Southern slaves migrated north, away from the increasing threat of violence (including lynchings), and away from broken promises of 40 acres of land and a mule for freed slave families. The ex-slaves journeyed to an industrialising urban north and carried the fragments of African cultural memory and the experience of slavery to cities like New York and Chicago to develop a new cultural invention of Black arts and imagination.

LEFT Master Juba performing at Vauxhall Gardens. Illustration from the *Illustrated London News*, 5 August 1848.

The exposure to European social norms, such as the dancing of the quadrille or the sound of marching bands and brass instruments, was inscribed into the African American experience and into American culture more widely. The fragments of African memory combined with European cultural practice morphed from generation to generation and went on to develop global cultures such as jazz and hip hop. Despite the unforgivable human brutality of slavery, a story of resistance, survival and the will of body and soul prevailed. African diaspora identity developed through a remix of cultures – African and European – that still filters through into today's dance floors. Minuets and the grand march lingered within the cakewalk, black bottom (see page 112) and Texas Tommy (see page 132) and ragtime became the 'in thing' on the dance floor.

Black dancers carried African movement with them throughout the history of slavery, their soulful dance marking the release and liberation within the African diaspora of both joy and pain that would later extend itself throughout the world to influence future dance forms. The bent and twisted shapes of the torso, arms and knees and the wild poses entwined within the African rhythms, which the Europeans did not understand, were seen as uncivilised.

However, these movements, unfamiliar to the Europeans, had meaning to the slaves, as a way to communicate instructions for escape and messages for survival or spiritual healing. These codes developed through African American dance and music, eventually going on to influence world culture such as hip hop.

The cakewalk first appeared around the mid-nineteenth century and was initially a plantation dance in which the slaves mocked their masters' dancing. It was likely a case of 'watching me watching you', with the slaves as confused by the plantation owners' dancing as the owners were by that of the slaves. The formality and the erect bodies of the Europeans dancing grand marches, cotillions, minuets and waltzes were then re-enacted by the slaves in competitions or as entertainment for the masters, performed in the hope that the best dancers would win a cake – hence, the cakewalk. The winning of the cake as a prize is said to be an Irish tradition, and may have come from Irish immigrants.[17]

The slaves' mimicry extended to dressing up in their masters' clothes and the dance was presented as couples strutting, elongating their walks and backs as caricatures of Europeans, but with African cool. Unfortunately as the cakewalk and Black social dances became

THIS PAGE 'Primrose & West's Big Minstrels: Our Great Champion Cake Walk, Open to All Comers'. Colour lithograph, c.1896.

OPPOSITE Sheet music for 'Little Missie Cakewalk': words by Talbot Owen, music by Montague Ring, with a Banjo Accompaniment (ad lib.) written by Clifford Essex, 1908.

...ILE MISSIE CAKEWALK

...ds by
...ot Owen

Music BY **MONTAGUE RING.**

With a Banjo Accompaniment (ad lib.)
Written by
CLIFFORD ESSEX.

...PYRIGHT 1908
...Y LUBLIN & Cº LTD.

Price 2/–net.

LONDON,
LUBLIN & Cº LTD.
83 Mortimer Street W.

C.G. RODER, LTD. LONDON.

popular in performance and competitions, much of its representation consisted of problematic caricatures of Black people as hypersexualised or with over-emphasised and comical features, often portrayed by white performers in blackface.

Dance does not require spoken language; it has its own physical language, though this can be perceived in a myriad of ways. It is often written that the European body is erect and the African body is bent from the knees. But beyond the postural analysis, between master and slave there were also differences in the movement, as well as the music being danced to; for the slaves the dancing European bodies would have been a strange and often comic sight. The slaves' mocking of the upright-dancing Europeans would develop into a popular dance of the early twentieth century: the cakewalk.

On 16 May 1903 at the Shaftesbury Theatre in London an all-Black American cast premièred *In Dahomey*, a musical comedy show that included cakewalks, starring George Walker and Bert Williams.[18] *In Dahomey* later went on to be performed at the Theatre Royal, Hull. In fact the cakewalk did not initially appear in the London run of *In Dahomey*, but was added to the show within in a week of its premiere by popular demand.

In Dahomey and its all-Black cast were seen as a genuine novelty and the show was perceived as a dramatic sensation because of the energised and comic performance of the cast. It received favourable reviews, though the language used was often derogatory towards Black people and the show was therefore seen more as minstrelised performance and Black spectacle than innovative musical theatre.[19] *In Dahomey* was also presented at Buckingham Palace at a party held for the ninth birthday of the future King Edward VII, then the Duke of Windsor.

By the late 1800s there were growing opportunities for African American self-expression through music, helped by increasing numbers of Black-only night clubs. African rhythms developed through piano or horn from slave spirituals and gospel through blues and ragtime and then into jazz. There were also local, informal places like the jook joints – after-hours spots where sexuality, liberation and creativity were played out by both Black and white people in different ways and for different reasons.[20] In these spaces Black people and the white working class were exploring their own ways of being away from the controlled dance spaces of the popular venues.

OPPOSITE 'The "Cake-Walk" and How to Dance It: A Chat with the Prima Donna of *In Dahomey*', from *Tatler*, 1 July 1903.

THE "CAKE-WALK" AND HOW TO DANCE IT

A Chat with the Prima Donna of "In Dahomey."

The "cake-walk," so popular in Paris in the early spring, has at length "caught on" here and appears to have "come to stay." The reason of its success is not far to seek, for this is a "boy-and-girl" season *par excellence* owing to the fact that there are now no fewer than four girl princesses at Court—Princesses Margaret and Patricia of Connaught, Princess Alice of Albany, and Princess Alice of Battenberg—and that any hostess who wishes to be in the running must of necessity give a ball for the young people. And certain it is that the young people all love the cake-walk. In *In Dahomey* at the Shaftesbury Theatre we are nightly seeing real negroes dancing the real cake-walk and noting the grace and true inwardness of the dance.

Quoth Ada Overton Walker, the leading lady at the Shaftesbury and the leading cake-walking exponent in New York, when asked by those seeking for the right inspiration years the cake became a smart affair, all icing and silver garnishing. Like the dance it has undergone changes, but both retain their first essential qualities.

In early days the dance was performed with greater dignity—was less of a dance and more of a walk. The Ethiop was in sooth a picturesque fellow. He went about his task with an inborn sense of beauty, handled his bale hooks with a flourish, thrummed his banjo with *chic*, and even managed to swing his pickaxe with a long and graceful swing. As for his wives and cousins and aunts they turned all in the dance to prettiness and to favour. And they still do. The English and American dancing of the cake-walk differ much as may be imagined from the original. In some houses it degenerates into a romp, but according to the expert its later development is all wrong. Joyousness should be tinged with sobriety.

steps may be practised. Some are very intricate; but the success of cake-walking depends largely on temperament, and as far as the actual steps are concerned the pupils may pass their instructors in time." The faces must be interested and joyous, and as the cake-walk is characteristic of a cheerful race to be properly appreciated it must be danced in the proper spirit—it is a gala dance.

In dancing all the muscles of the body are brought into play, any effort or fatigue is concealed, the shoulders thrown well back, the back curved, and the knees bent with suppleness. The swing, all jauntiness and graceful poise, must come from the shoulders, and the toes must turn well out. The *tempo* is between that of the two-step and the march six-eight time. The negro melodies which may be played for the dancers are without number. In the quicker number the women should be careful to manage their

THE "CAKE-WALK" AS DANCED AT THE SHAFTESBURY THEATRE IN THE NIGGER MUSICAL COMEDY, "IN DAHOMEY"
The dancers are Mr. Salsbury and Miss Davies

Campbell & Gray

in the dance: "Sunshine in your hearts. Think of moonlight nights and pine knots and tallow dips, and of lives untouched by the hardness of toil, for I tell you there was sunshine in the hearts of those who first danced the cake-walk."

The cake-walk has traces of the African dances of centuries ago, and in the Southern States of America was developed into an art long before the Civil War. Always looked upon as a festival dance, it was danced by the negroes in celebration of any happy occasion—a wedding, a name day, the end of cotton picking or corn shucking, or anything which gave cause for jollity. Moonlight nights were always chosen, if possible, for the merrymaking; but if the moon proved inconstant lighted pine knots and tallow dips were pressed into the service. The cake was made of cornmeal finely crushed, baked in the ashes of the remains of a gipsy fire, and ornamented with cabbage leaves. In later

Horseplay should be done away with for good and all. Dance wisely but not too well, and be sure to let the source of fun be wholly untinged with vulgarity."

The cake-walk is executed by a man and woman. The latter should impress his partner with the grace of his walking, and she charm him with her subtle grace and coquetry. The man depends upon the woman and the woman upon the man for the prospects of winning the prize.

"It is difficult," confides Mrs. Walker, the high priestess, "to call the steps of the cake-walk by name." In the walk you follow the music, and as you keep time with it in what is best defined as a march you improvise. Gestures, evolutions, poses, will come to you as you go through the dance. The partners may develop steps which they think will impress the judges. Every muscle must be in perfect control. The step of the cake-walk is light and elastic; after it has been learned fancy

long skirts gracefully, an art which requires a good deal of practice, and beginners do well to wear the shorter skirts.

The cake-walk may be danced by any number of couples. A tall couple leads off, holding up the hands as in a barn dance. A cake is placed in the centre of the room on a pedestal, the opening bars of the music are played, and the dancers march round. The walk over, with its various features, its impromptu steps, and gaiety coming to an end, the question arises, "Who takes the cake?" The couples now march round in all solemnity and bow to the cake *en passant*. A halt at command when every couple has passed by. Then the master of the ceremonies names the winners. The cake is carried before them by the master or one of the guests, two lines are formed of the dancers, and the happy couple dance between the lines to general hand-clapping. So ends the cake-dance.

CONSTANCE BEERBOHM.

Animal dances such as the grizzly bear, where you reached out your arms and hung them over your partner's shoulders, mimicking the movements of a dancing bear, were to rule the dance floor. Along with the grizzly bear, many other dances of the time including the bunny hug, camel walk, turkey trot and pigeon walk featured ragtime rhythms.[21]

New dances exploded into the early twentieth century, and the Roaring Twenties and Prohibition brought new rebellions. A fresh generation of women, given the name flappers,[22] broke with accepted fashion by wearing what were considered short skirts and having short, bobbed hair. They provided a statement of early twentieth-century womanhood then considered brash and a flouting of social order by drinking alcohol, smoking cigarettes, driving cars, partaking in casual sex and – of course – listening to jazz.

The United States and Europe brought different meanings to ragtime. The speakeasies in the United States were places of intrigue, danger and daring dances, while Europe set out to both embrace and manage the new rhythms and dances of ragtime by quietening them down into a more civilised recreation. Soon the tango and foxtrot would follow suit (see pages 62 and 78). Spanning the 1920s, the Harlem Renaissance was a flowering of Black urban social expression centred on Harlem in New York City. Music, dance, art, literature, fashion and thought exploded into and challenged popular culture. The downtown white elite were drawn to places like the Cotton Club to watch the Black entertainers, with names such as Cab Calloway, Josephine Baker and the Nicholas Brothers taking centre stage. However, discrimination was still being played out every night as they performed to a racially segregated, white-only audience.

The injustice of segregated audiences and performers in the Cotton Club is mind-numbing. As a performer I cannot comprehend the breath one would need to take night after night as one entered the stage – and yet it remains a courageous act for Black performers even in the twenty-first century. The African diaspora body has taken many different shapes since slavery. The merging of European and African dance forms and musical cultures has gifted us many ways to dance, through a potent mix of both the most tragic and the most beautiful human experiences, where dances conceal within them human history.

OPPOSITE Sheet music for 'The Bunny Hug', words by William Jerome, music by Harry Von Tilzer, 1912.

No. 561, MARCH 27, 1912]   THE TATLER

TERPSICHOREAN TERRORS
Which are Threatening to Undermine the Decorum of Our Ballrooms.

THE GRIZZLY BEAR

In this dance the partners perform all sorts of startling gyrations. One figure is a very long walking-hopping step interrupted at intervals by a series of violent twists that are amazing

THE BUNNY HUG

The partners dance unusually close in a slow gliding step, slightly swaying the bodies to the right and left in time with the music

THE TURKEY TROT

In this figure the man dances close and directly in front of his partner, bending forward a trifle with his hands on his hips. His attitude is that of one in the act of stealing a kiss

THE TANGO

The above photograph illustrates a glide in one of the variations of the Turkey Trot known as the Tango. The man keeps slightly behind his partner

The above snapshots show those much-discussed dances, the Bunny Hug, Turkey Trot, etc., as actually danced in New York, the home of their origin

355

ABOVE 'Terpsichorean Terrors Which are Threatening to Undermine the Decorum of Our Ballrooms', from *Tatler*, 27 March 1912. Dancers demonstrate the grizzly bear, bunny hug, turkey trot and tango.

The Agony of Terpsichore

CONTEMPLATING THE LATEST DEVELOPMENT OF HER ART

THE TURKEY TROT—IN FOUR PHASES

Above are photographs of the latest aberration of the dance craze. The performers (Oscar and Suzette, at the Hippodrome) are indulging in what is known as "The Turkey Trot." Opinions may possibly differ as to the grace and charm of this new excursion, but Terpsichore surely would disown the innovation as having no relation to her great art. The background to the photograph was drawn by Mr. Charles Sykes

ABOVE 'The Agony of Terpsichore Contemplating the Latest Development of Her Art', from the *Bystander*, 21 February, 1912. Oscar and Suzette demonstrate the turkey trot at the London Hippodrome. A distressed Terpsichore, the muse of dance, reflects how it divided popular opinion at the time.

DANCING IN TIME · AMERICAN RHYTHMS, AFRICAN BEATS

THE RAGTIME DANCE

WORDS AND MUSIC
BY

Scott Joplin

Composer of
MAPLE LEAF RAG,
SUNFLOWER SLOW DRAG,
SWIPESY CAKE WALK,
PEACHERINE RAG.

75

PUBLISHED BY

JOHN STARK & SON
SHEET MUSIC PUBLISHERS
ST. LOUIS, MO.

The cakewalk, like the grizzly bear, became a victim of changing social tastes and soon disappeared, to be replaced by the next dance fad. As tastes changed, African American dances were shared and cross-pollinated into the social dance world, bringing in new actors and opportunities. The famed dances of Vernon (1887–1918) and Irene (1893–1969) Castle in the early twentieth century are part of that history.[23] The Castles, a white couple based in New York (although Vernon was English), brought many African American dances to the fore, such as the turkey trot, albeit a smoother version of it that suited their brand.[24]

The couple's signature dance was the Castle walk – a slow, stylised partner dance based on a one-step (a partner dance with simple steps to the beat of the music often incorporating a turn). The Castles were very much influencers of both fashion and dance in their time; Fred Astaire (1899–1987) and Ginger Rogers (1911–1995) would star in their screen biopic, *The Story of Vernon and Irene Castle* (1939). Astaire had once been a student of the Castles and achieved a stardom that lives on today, an opportunity not given to the Castles as they were famous before the talkies.

Irene Castle was known as much for her short, cropped hair and fashion sense as for her dancing. As well as being an advocate for animal rights she was ahead of her time in many other ways. The Castles' fondness for animals saw them gather a virtual menagerie of animals: cats, dogs and horses, along with a succession of monkeys. They often took their pets, including a monkey or two, on tour. The Castles were the darlings of the in-crowd in both North America and Europe. They debuted the latest dances, and performed on stage in clubs and at the most exclusive parties.

The Castles were much in demand as teachers, charging high fees as well as having a remarkably busy performing schedule. They typically performed in the theatre, often with more than one stage performance a day, then went on to dance in clubs into the early hours, all in addition to teaching dance during the day. They became a brand with off-shoots that included clothing and instructional dance manuals.

OPPOSITE Sheet music for 'The Ragtime Dance', words and music by Scott Joplin, 1903.

THIS PAGE Advertisement for 'The Famous Cotton Club presents Dan Healy's ... *Cotton Club on Parade* with Cab Calloway and his famous Cotton Club Orchestra', 1925.

THIS PAGE Score for 'The Castle Walk: Trot & One Step', composed by James Reese Europe and Ford T. Dabney, 1914.

OPPOSITE Photograph of Vernon and Irene Castle by Frances Benjamin Johnston, c.1912.

The financial reward for the Castles was great, but their lives were blighted by excessive spending and bad investments. Vernon died tragically on 15 February 1918[25] at the age of 30 in an aeroplane crash near Fort Worth, Texas. He had joined the Royal Flying Corps in 1916, his interest in dancing having waned and feeling that being part of the war effort was the right thing to do. Irene mostly retired from dancing after Vernon's death and went on to work in silent films and increase her animal-rights activism, founding an animal shelter in Illinois called Orphans of the Storm. She died in 1969 at the age of 75.

Within the many dances that the Castles brought to the world, as with other white performers and dance teachers of that time, was a balance of cultural transmission and appropriation. Black social dances were taken and adapted to suit white consumers, enabling dancers such as the Castles to have a career unavailable to Black dancers. This lack of opportunity stemmed from the racist simultaneous perception of Black culture as capital but Black people as inferior – a reality of appropriation still present today.

Beneath the popular dance culture was the underground scene, with dance spots like the Hoofers Club in Harlem during the Harlem Renaissance. A small room only 10 by 6 metres in size, with a piano in the corner, it was a legendary after-hours club where dancers such as tap-dancing duos the Nicholas Brothers and the Berry Brothers and solo tappers such as Bill Robinson or Baby Laurence went to jam. It was also a place where such famed and aspiring dancers would share and compete in dance steps against each other. The Hoofers Club was small but seldom humble, its motto being 'survive or die'.

You could say American rhythm is the call and response, both ghost and future projection of popular culture. Ancient rhythms have carved musical and dance innovation that echoes backwards and forwards, absorbing and influencing many different forms of dance and popular culture. These rhythms draw both competition and togetherness and bring an endless gift of expression to the dance floor, rhythms that from ragtime gave us jazz, rhythm and blues, rock 'n' roll, funk, soul, hip hop, house, disco and so much more. This is music that has captivated generations on the dance floor and got people dancing all around the world.

OPPOSITE Photograph of Bill Robinson by Carl Van Vechten, 1933.

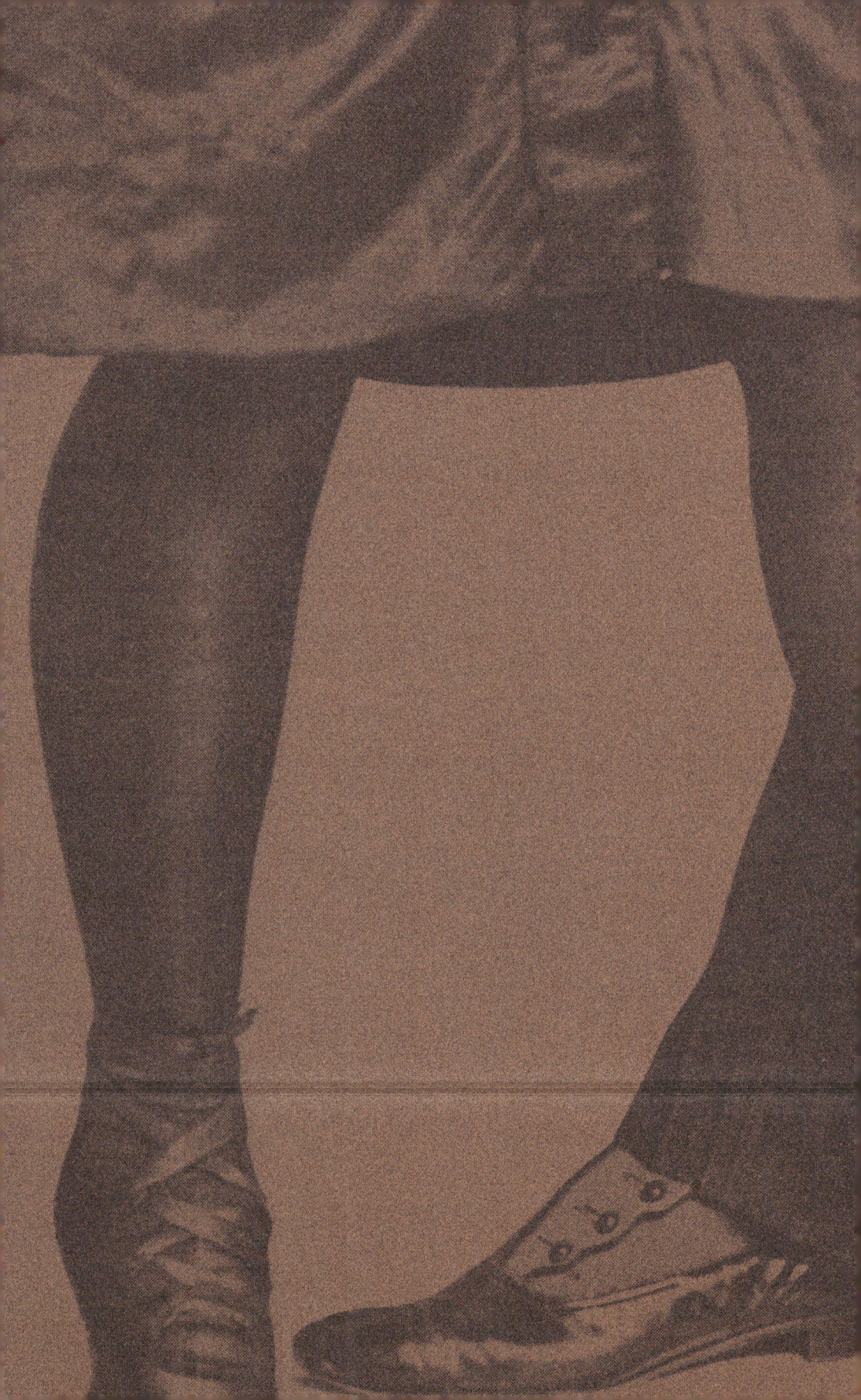

CHAPTER 03

THE TANGO

THE TANGO ORIGINATED in Argentina in the late nineteenth century, born out of the *bordellos* (brothels) and *arrabales* – slums and dockland areas, such as San Telmo, by the River Plate in Buenos Aires. Further back than that its origins stretch beyond Argentina to Cuba, Uruguay and Africa. Tango is a patchwork of dances with its roots in the rhythms and movements of *candombe*,[26] a dance from Montevideo in neighbouring Uruguay. *Candombe* is a solo and group-based African ritual dance in which dancers seek to be possessed by divine spirits. Like many other dances of the time, *candombe* merged African rhythms and movement with European partner-based dances like the mazurka to form the tango.[27] This process was similar to that with the cakewalk, developed through mimicry of European dance steps: a dance born out of the circumstances of its time – of slavery, migration and colonialism.

Along with the *candombe*, another dance that added to the patchwork of tango was the *milonga*, which carries traces of both Cuban influences and the Czech dance the polka, and which is also the name given to a place where dancers gather. Newly arrived Italian immigrants to Argentina also built subtle layers into the dance that would later become tango, threading the African rhythms with traces of opera within the music, along with Spanish Catalan rhythms that held traces of Moorish harmonies. Another dance called *canyengue*,[28] which pre-dates the tango we know today, originated from Kongo people, from Central Africa, who had been taken as slaves. It is similar to the tango but with a faster pace. *Canyengue* is translated as 'melt to the music', or step it down, start to party. That phrase alone, 'melt to the music', captures the idea of tango perfectly.

The popular story of tango is one that begins with dock workers and lonely immigrants from Europe: Italians, Spaniards and migrant Jews from Poland or Russia, looking for female companionship, who frequented the brothels and salons of Buenos Aires where the owners hired bands to play for patrons. In late nineteenth-century Buenos Aires men far outnumbered women, although there are conflicting estimates of the exact male-to-female ratio. One source says that men outnumbered women 170 to 100.[29] Another thought is 100 to one.[30] There is even an estimate of five men to one woman.[31] These numbers paint a picture of a tragic place where love was nigh-on unobtainable, but there is also the theory of some scholars that the numbers grew out of middle-class propaganda about tango and the bordellos intended to separate the tango of the middle and upper classes from that of the

OPPOSITE 'Dancing People: Candombe', oil painting by Pedro Figari, c.1920.

prostitutes and dockers of Buenos Aires,[32] whom they thought of as uncivilised.

Prostitution and brothels became an unwelcome reality for the middle and upper classes, and they engineered a more civilised tango or salon scene in the following years, both to gentrify tango and to distract from the visits of some members of the upper and middle classes to the brothels and bars.[33] Surely a classic case of 'do as I say, not as I do'. *Milongas* evolved into more refined dancing places where people could gather to dance tango in a more socially appealing environment that attracted a broader community all the family could enjoy, and where the middle classes could comfortably frame their idea of Argentinian society.

Tango is a narrative of a people finding themselves in a strange land: *gauchos* – Argentinian cowboys who had relocated to the docks and city to look for work – sailors and dock workers looking for love, and women, born in Argentina or part of the influx of European immigrants arriving to help build a new world, found themselves in a still-forming industrial metropolis. *Compadritos* meanwhile were street-wise young men who came from the overpopulated *conventillos* – tenements and *arrabales* on the outskirts of the city. These early proponents of the tango were proud and macho, with a zest for violence. Their trademark or gang uniform was a white neckerchief tied around the neck and a wide-brimmed hat worn loosely to cover one eye, high-heeled boots and a knife hanging from the hip.[34] *Compadritos* would hang around the seedier parts of Buenos Aires, near to the bars and brothels where tango developed.

For women lawful employment was scarce, one reason some turned to prostitution. Immigrant women from Europe arriving in Buenos Aires could be faced with forced prostitution from pimps or hustlers. Rumours of white slavery[35] crossed continents and created fear and speculation about the potential fate of European women in Buenos Aires. With no community of their own to protect them these women could be prey for opportunistic men, and for some the good life they had sought on the other side of the world was anything but.

Sexual frustration and desire can be difficult to escape. In many ways desire encompasses what tango is: a dance of sexuality, passion,

promise and pleasure. One can imagine that the competition to attract female attention, even momentarily, would have been a high-level game. Good dancing and the tango in particular were prized as much as money. They were your calling card, an initial introduction that ensured female attention or at least got you noticed. Machismo did of course come into play too.[36] Tango was pushed away from its rhythmic origins and towards the hyper-heterosexual: men with puffed-up chests plotting, posturing and even fighting for female attention.[37] This led to a stereotype of hyper-macho tango, which was appropriated by Hollywood and became a distraction from the complexity and beauty of tango as it favoured machismo over the sophistication of its movements.

Another side to the tango story is of men dancing tango together to hone their skills and impress potential female partners.[38] Given that dance was a valued currency for pleasure, wanting to know tango and do it well makes sense. In the present the idea of dockworkers dancing tango together, possibly directing their sexuality towards one another, may seem unexpected. This of course depends on where it is being danced. For example if Compton Street, a well-known destination for gay men in Soho, London, was the scene of a tango street party, the sight of men dancing with other men and enjoying

the music would likely not raise an eyebrow. On the other hand if men in a traditionally heterosexual environment were to dance tango together, say at half-time of a football match, it might seem strange to some. Of course in the twenty-first century queer tango is very visible.[39] Who is to say it was not one hundred years ago? The images of men dancing tango together in its early form most often seem to tell a story of necessity more than anything else, though maybe the men dancing tango together in nineteenth-century Buenos Aires just liked to dance with one another. Dance is dance is dance.

Tango eventually found its way into the wider world of the United States and Europe. It was a new dance that seduced

OPPOSITE Photograph labelled 'Reunion de cocheros, 1906'.

THIS PAGE Score for 'The Argentine (Tango-Dance)', from *The Sunshine Girl*, music by Paul A. Rubens, 1912.

the awaiting in-crowd with its sense of the erotic. Compared to the folk dances and *contredanses* of old that featured distance and proper behaviour and where close dancing and body contact were considered scandalous or immoral, here was a dancing statement that made no attempt to be proper – tango must have been quite a shock to many. It was met with outrage from many quarters including Catholic and Episcopal bishops, who struggled with tango to the point that in its early development in Europe in 1914 Cardinal Basilio Pompili, the Vicar General of Rome, wrote a vehement letter condemning the tango to *L'Osservatore Romano*, the newspaper of the Vatican state that reports on the daily events of the Church. Pope Pius X had to tone it down before it could be published.[40]

In 1924 tango was introduced to the Catholic Church in a much gentler and even fitting way by El Vasco Aín (1874–1940) from Buenos Aires. Aín, at the age of 50, danced for Pope Pius XI in the Vatican Library on an occasion arranged by the Argentine Embassy.[41] Dressed in tails, with his partner in a long, dark-blue skirt, he proceeded to present a tango to the Pope. The accompanying music was Francisco Canaro's tango 'Ave Maria', which was thought to be a diplomatic choice of music for the Pope. The pair are said to have danced a moderate tango with less

of the close embrace that they normally danced, and they gave only a hint of the sensuality of tango. Aín, who learnt the dance on the streets of Buenos Aires and was used to a more passionate and dramatic tango, with much closer and more sensuous holds, demonstrated two real unfiltered movements from his street tango near the end of the dance by making a small run with his partner and finishing in a freeze. The Pope was said to be pleased.[42]

Tango first appeared in the British press in 1911[43] and by 1912–13 had hit its peak in Britain. In Paris tango became the favoured fashionable pastime for the elite, following a similar dance, named apache – later tango apache – which caught the eye of Parisian society. Part dance, part melodrama, it re-enacted a physical argument in a bar between a pimp wearing a stripy T-shirt and a prostitute clad in a slit skirt and suspenders.[44]

The performance of apache could have been quite comical if it weren't for the very physical mock slaps, violent lifts and throwing of the woman to the floor. It borders more on performance and cabaret than social dance and is less suited to the twenty-first-century eye in its earliest versions. This is a bar-room brawl told through dance with realities that have touches of Pina Bausch

OPPOSITE 'How to Dance the Valentino Tango', front cover to *Girls' Cinema*, 13 October 1923.

BEAUTIFUL OMAR PEARL NECKLACES — FOR — SEE SIMPLE COM-
READERS! PETITION INSIDE

GIRLS' CINEMA

Long Complete Novel Inside

EVERY TUESDAY

No. 157. Vol. 7.
Oct. 13, 1923.

2d

How to Dance *the* Valentino Tango

Article Inside

(1940–2009) about its performance. Bausch was a German choreographer famous for highly dramatic modern dance works that explore psychological trauma and human relationships. In a similar way, apache shows the human potential for violence. Its raw, more primal beginnings did not last the test of time, thankfully.

Tango's arrival in Europe provided a new dancing playground for high society. It was an opportunity to stylishly occupy the dance floor with sexual promise, entwined bodies, flicking, crossing, cutting legs, strong holds, seductive poses and dancing flirtation. Sexuality danced both in dark corners and in open spaces where the presence of seduction and desire were sought. Close proximity and bodies touching, teasing and wanting were on the menu.

Tango tea dances proved to be a big hit from the early twentieth century. Regular tango tea dances were held at grand places such as the Waldorf Hotel in London, which hosted tea dances as early as 1908, complete, of course, with neatly cut sandwiches, savouries and warm scones. These famed events were stylish affairs where champagne, tea or any beverage of choice could be sipped while the tango was danced. Demonstrations and dance lessons were also available to keep high society up to date with the latest moves. There were other tea dances that favoured more Latin styles of dance and, if one wanted a late dance, tango suppers were also available on the social calendars of high society and the dancing enthusiasts of the day.

Usually a live band accompanied the dancing and sometimes a phonograph was on hand to play the latest hot tunes. Tea dances proved popular in the United States and Europe and remained so until just after the Second World War, when the interest of dancing enthusiasts wandered elsewhere – in particular to the jitterbug. The Waldorf held its tango tea dances until 1939, stopping only when a German bomb shattered the glass roof of the Palm Court where the dances were held. In 1982 the Waldorf re-established its famous tea dances, which still run today.

ABOVE Photograph of Molasso and Corio, dance team in apache-type costume and pose, c.1909.

OPPOSITE 'El Tango Tragico' performed by Marjorie Moss and Georges Fontana' from the *Bystander*, 23 July 1924.

The Sketch

No. 1085.—Vol. LXXXIV.   WEDNESDAY, NOVEMBER 12, 1913.   SIXPENCE.

WHY WORRY ABOUT HOME RULE AND THE LAND QUESTION WHEN YOU CAN LEARN THE TANGO?
A STEP FROM THE CRAZE-DANCE OF THE MOMENT.

Everybody's doing the Tango, learning the Tango, talking the Tango, or watching the Tango. Never, perhaps, has a dance become of such universal interest so quickly — despite "A Peeress" and others, who deem it negroid—and partly, perhaps, because of the publicity they gave it. As all our readers no doubt know, the dance went to the British ball-room from the stage, as it went also to the restaurant. To the British stage it came, by way of the Continent, from the Argentine, of which it is a 400-year-old national dance. It may be added, by the way, that the original dance has at least two hundred steps ; for ball-room purposes about five-and-twenty are all that is necessary. As a second " by the way," let us say that the Tango tea may be said to have invaded even the Prussian Parliament, which is not, as a rule, given to lightness of heart—or of feet. All of which is to say that the other day the wife of the President of the Diet lent her official apartments to the hosts of a Tango tea.

Photograph by Illustrations Bureau.

Miss Swepstone & Mr. Tweedale
in a Dance Figure

OPPOSITE 'Why worry about home rule and the land question, when you can learn the tango?' Front cover to *The Sketch*, 12 November 1913. It shows the entwined legs of two dancers performing the tango.

THIS PAGE *How to Dance the Tango ... and other popular dances*, described by Miss Eileen Swepstone and Mr. Bernard Tweedale, illustrated by Miss Swepstone, 1914.

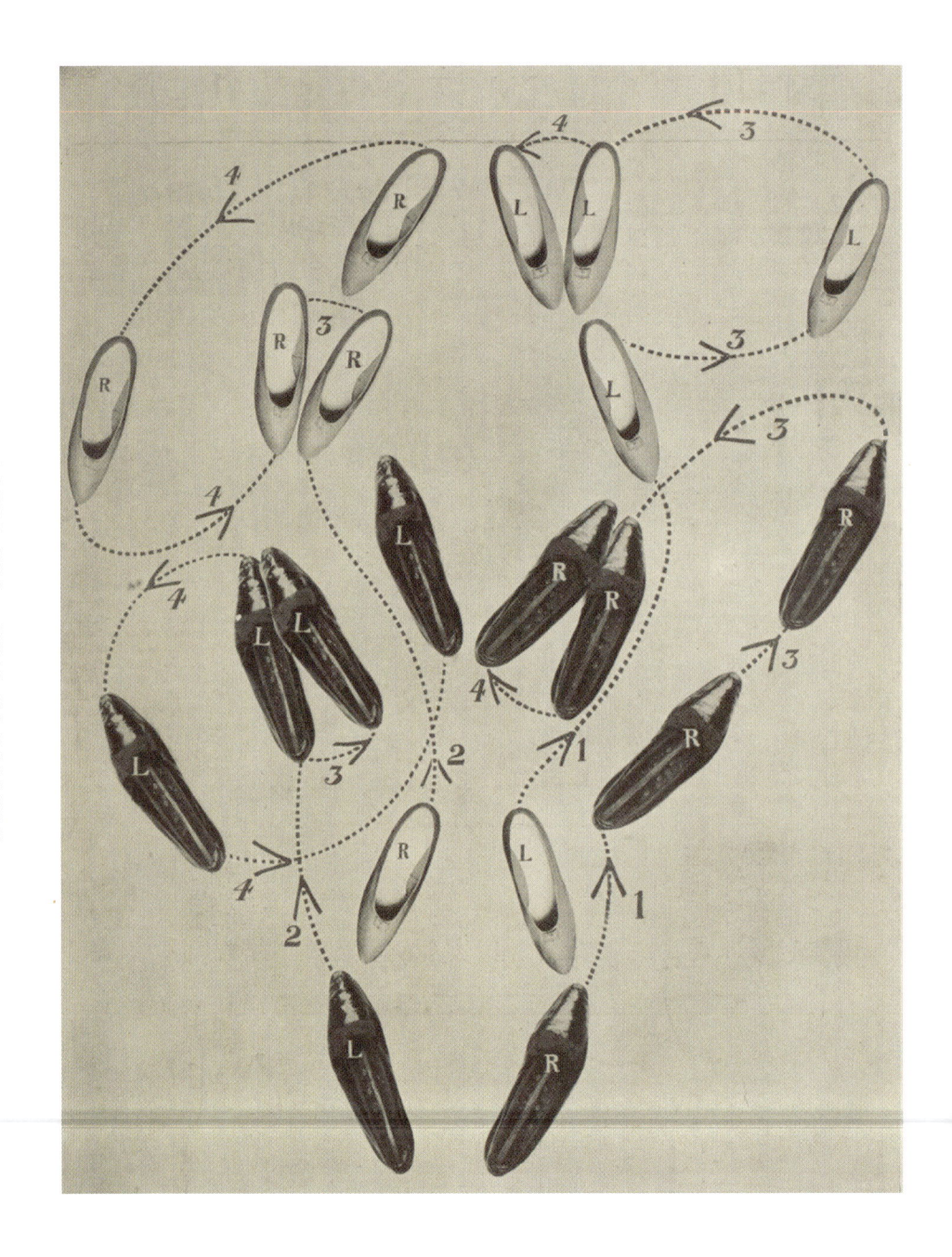

Tango's popularity fluctuated in Argentina from the 1940s. There was a tango resurgence in the mid-1940s and 1950s under the presidency of Juan and First Lady Eva Perón, as the working class became financially better off and leisure was more affordable. However, political instability and a military coup in 1955 rendered Argentina fragile and curfews were imposed. Nightlife became a thing of the past and many of the dance halls became abandoned and disused.[45] Beyond Argentina the 1950s ushered in a new age of dancing and rock 'n' roll appeared, bringing an American voice to the latest music and dance trends that changed the dance floor for a new generation. All around the world, dance halls and ballrooms saw the demise of live music as vinyl records and the drift towards individual dancing like the twist took its place; tango slid into the shadows.

The film *Last Tango in Paris* (1972), starring Marlon Brando, did less for tango than the name suggests. Marlon Brando and his co-star Maria Schneider danced a tango (loosely put) in a film that prioritised machismo and sexuality over the dance itself. It is a Hollywood cross-over of cultural disconnection and dance fads that serves

choreography in second place to the framing and reputation of the actors. Instead of the *bordellos* where tango began, the focus was on close-ups of the actors' faces. Rudolph Valentino (1895–1926) was the first to utilise tango's popularity on the big screen,[46] aligning himself with a sense of machismo and a gaucho's gaze with the popular dance style, and extending a stereotype that would haunt tango for years.

In the 1980s Argentina sought to rebuild itself and the connection of dance with politics was visible once again. Tango was welcomed by the state as a signifier of Argentinian culture and slowly absorbed into the national identity. Now tango was both cultural and economic currency, a familiar story throughout this book. A dance once seen as uncivilised was embraced and nationalised – tango shifted from being a community that dances to being a business and financial opportunity.

OPPOSITE 'A Tango Tangle', from *The Sketch*, 26 November 1913. 'Some small notion of the intricacy of the dance may be gained from this diagram of the seventh figure, showing el cruzado cortado and le croise coupe'.

THIS PAGE 'Tango dancing at Harewood Place, a newly opened venue for the tango tea craze of 1913', from *The Sphere*, 29 November 1913.

Tango, like many popular dances, was able to shake off the glitz and glamour of its past and reform itself through communities with a legitimate passion for the dance. No cameras, no Hollywood: just taking it back to the source. This elevated tango satisfied a new generation and audience, who could see tango in many shapes and forms around the world, from dance classes to performances in big theatre venues and local clubs. In the 2000s, the critically acclaimed and award-winning Argentinian dance company Tango Fire toured the world, bringing tango to new theatre audiences.

Speaking as a performer, I find that when you are on stage, being sensual is the last thing on your mind. Often the technical aspects of potentially dangerous lifts and reading your partner's movement and gentle nudges that signal weight transitions and oncoming lifts take over from any thoughts of love. But who is to say that the love we see in staged performance is not real? Tango as social dance is very different from staged performance; it is unpredictable and unscripted. Performance is about fantasy and while some relationships may project an artificial love, others may not. In tango potential love is played out in social settings and that is what makes it special.

At its core tango is primal theatre, a fantasy that opens the imagination to sex. It is not artificial, but a play of real emotions performed in social spaces. Tango is both delicate and forceful; a visceral, stylish play of bodies commenting, teasing, opposing,

maybe letting in, maybe not. I find the legwork of tango inspiring – the neat cuts, angles and shapes of the legs as readable as text that tells the inner story of the dancers. Tango holds so much drama and, despite the fact that for most it is a social dance, it requires an attention to detail and commitment to performance that many a professional dancer would strive for. A dance of improvisation, skill and emotion that requires shared thought and bodies, tango has its own rules, nuance and history – its own dancing universe.

Dancing tango in tango salons is organised through *tandas*,[47] where partners dance together for three or four songs to a live band or recorded music. A short break of up to a minute then occurs when the unwritten rule allows time to change dancing partners. Often pre-set eye signals or nods are the unspoken ways to arrange your next dance partner, allowing for dancers to accept or decline an offer. Wholly unlike stage performances, in these games of real life, looks of dismissal or allure unfold spontaneously in both body and eyes as sensual play towards the potential of a sexual encounter between the partners.

Tango in the present day is a refined, sensuous dance – a dance of skill and style, of seduction and secret liaisons – that still holds the sexual rawness of its past. It is a dance of love (whether real or imagined); whatever the reason for dancing, it still takes two to tango.

OPPOSITE Sketches by Helen McKie made at the tea tango at the Olympia Salle de Danse in Paris, from the *Bystander*, 19 November 1913.

HELEN McKIE

CHAPTER 04

FOXTROTS AND FIERCE COMPETITION

THE FOXTROT IS thought to have begun with Harry Fox (1882–1959), an African American vaudeville entertainer, in the early 1900s in the United States. He first developed the dance when entertaining audiences in between movie shows. His interludes would contain comedy gags and dancing girls named the American Beauties; at the time sexualised dancing in performances was banned, so Fox, along with many other entertainers, would find other ways to stimulate his audience. One method was to stage the dancers in a series of tableaux – a freeze-frame of poses that would allow an audience the opportunity to appreciate their beauty and make for a raunchier show that would nontheless not attract the attention of the authorities.[48]

Fox took what was a slow walk on two beats and made it into a one trot – one step per beat, in which he would trot around the stage – which later developed into the partner dance. This allowed him to move around freely and position himself in between two of the American Beauties, where he would tell jokes with the girls in pose as his backdrop. The foxtrot became part of his show when he performed in the Ziegfeld Follies Cabaret in New York and quickly spread throughout the United States and beyond. It is a smooth partner dance characterised by long, flowing movements similar to those of the waltz, and it proved to be a great accompaniment to the sounds of ragtime.

Britain was first introduced to the foxtrot in the summer of 1914 at the 400 Club on Bond Street in London and the fashionable tea dances held at Harewood Place[49] in Mayfair, go-to events for high society in London at that time. Such venues offered the women in their long, flowing dresses and the men in their tie and tails a place where they could add a twist of English decadence and flair to the popular American dances. Quite possibly the foxtrot was also danced in places other than those frequented by the social elite in London.

The foxtrot became an immediate hit, yet with its popularity came criticism. The foxtrot, like many of its predecessors, was to be called a shameless dance, vulgar and a threat to social norms. Unlike the minuets, quadrilles and other dances of the past, the foxtrot was simple in steps and easy to learn. The one-step, which involved single steps to the beat of the music, must have seemed quite slow compared to the foxtrot – maintaining the same pace or tempo all evening was surely uninspired labour after a while. The foxtrot had a more playful rhythm and enabled the dancers to express themselves more freely. It offered simplicity along with the syncopated beats of ragtime and contemporary tempos that gave dancers a new energy, one they could identify as their own.

OPPOSITE Sheet music for 'Hello, Frisco! Fox Trot', a song from the *Ziegfeld Follies*, lyrics by Gene Buck, music by Louis A. Hirsch, 1915.

In the early part of the twentieth century ragtime and animal dances signalled things to come for the dance floor. The coded mannerisms of the nineteenth century gave way to a freer improvisational dance experience, where mimicry such as acting out the movements of a grizzly bear was seen as a lot more fun than the dances of yesteryear for a youthful dance floor and the new in-crowd. Men could now avoid previous formalities when inviting women to dance, and dance cards, detailing the pre-arranged and ordered list of dancing suitors, were cast aside. The foxtrot no doubt gave moments of liberation to the dancers of the early twentieth century. As the First World War approached, dance made some lives a little easier. It may sound romantic, but dance heals and it costs nothing: it's an escape.

Not only was the foxtrot the 'in thing', but it also brought opportunities. Dance competitions and major events dedicated to the foxtrot ensued and commercial opportunity inevitably followed. Josephine Bradley (1893–1985) was a leading dance teacher who became famous after winning many foxtrot dance competitions. One such, organised at the Embassy Club in 1920, Bradley won with her partner, the American dancer G. K. Anderson. Owing to her many achievements Bradley was affectionately known as the First Lady of ballroom dancing in her time.

The popularity of the foxtrot and the relative ease with which one could learn the basic steps meant dance manuals and notated dance steps became widely available for those who wanted to keep up with the latest developments. But notation as a way to teach or record dance has always been a complex process. The structure and framework of musical notation are more straightforward, with an accepted set of conventions that are widely used, while dance notation is in some ways still being figured out – even today. From stick people, dots or footsteps on the floor to Laban notation – a series of symbols developed by the Hungarian dance artist Rudolf Laban (1879–1958) to notate dance[51] – a general agreement on a single organising principal of dance notation is yet to be arrived at.

Despite these challenges, in the early to mid-twentieth century carefully drawn steps and detailed instructions on new dances were printed and sold in large quantities. Learning these floor plans of dancing offered the chance to improve your dance ability, and perhaps your social position. British ballrooms, as well as many others around the world, were filled with those whose knowledge of the dance steps had come from freshly printed paper. Dancing entrepreneurs such as the famed English band leader and dancer Victor Silvester (1900–1978)[52] and Vernon and Irene Castle developed dance classes and produced

OPPOSITE 'Where Débutantes Dance: Fox-trotting at the Florida', plate from *Nights in London: Where Mayfair Makes Merry* by Horace Wyndham, 1926. Illustration by Dorothea St John George.

dance manuals and music for those who wanted to do dance the proper way. Printed dance tutorials became a profitable arm of dance teaching, as a companion business to physical tuition. They mirrored the success of the song sheets produced by Tin Pan Alley: print was big business.

Arthur Murray (1895–1991) was born in Hungary but his family moved to America when he was 2 years old. Murray became a ballroom dancer and businessman and went on to take dance to the masses in an ambitious way, building his own dance studio chain and franchise system across the United States, Britain and around the world. The young Arthur Murray first took dance classes in New York and in 1915 started tuition with Vernon and Irene Castle in tango and the Castle walk. Murray went on to forge new pathways in social dance by publishing a series of dance manuals, such as *How to Become a Good Dancer*[53] and *The Modern Dances*.[54] He became a great advocate for ballroom dance and teaching, and his dance manuals were famous for the carefully structured footprints that guided would-be dancers in learning dances such as the foxtrot.

Like his teachers before him Murray took Black social dances and popularised them

in his own studio system, often giving little or no credit to their background. In 1939 his popularity exploded through his introduction of the Big Apple (see page 114) and the Lambeth Walk. The Lambeth Walk was popularised in the musical *Me and My Girl* (1937) and took its name from Lambeth Walk, a street in South London once known for its market. It is a dance that exaggerates the cheeky-chappy strut to be seen in South London working streets. Between 1950 and 1960 Arthur Murray took dance to television on his show *The Arthur Murray Party*, which aired the latest dances as well as proving to be a great advertisement for his dance studio chain. In 1964 Arthur Murray sold the chain and at present the

OPPOSITE Score for 'Ève Fox-Trot', from a two-act revue, *Paris qui Jazz*, by Albert Willemetz, performed at the Casino de Paris, 1920.

THIS PAGE Photograph of Josephine Bradley dancing with her husband, from *Dancing through Life: An Autobiography*, 1947.

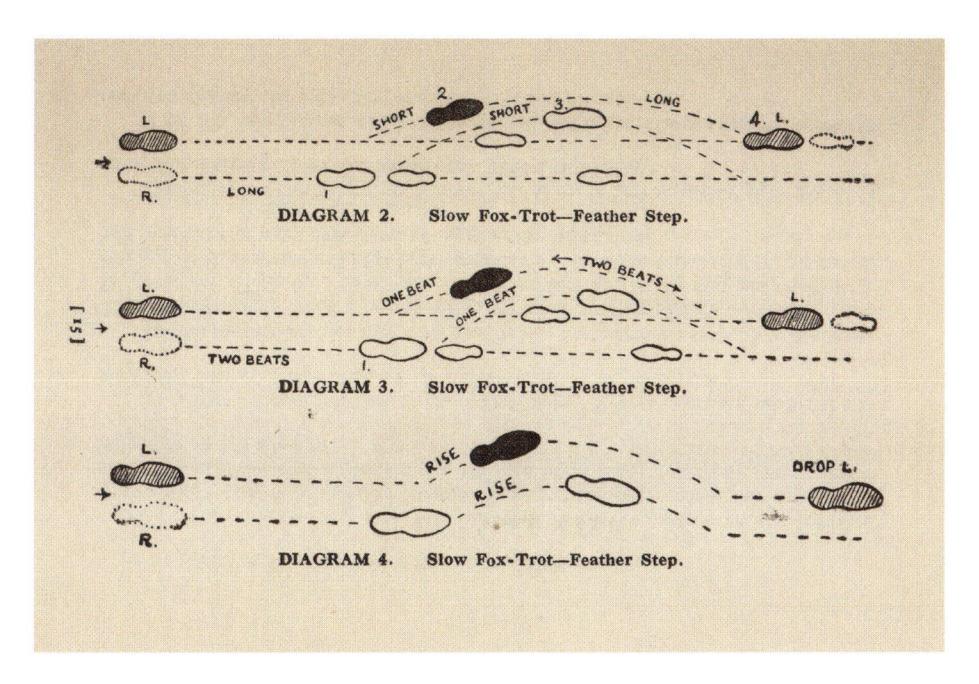

DIAGRAM 2.   Slow Fox-Trot—Feather Step.

DIAGRAM 3.   Slow Fox-Trot—Feather Step.

DIAGRAM 4.   Slow Fox-Trot—Feather Step.

OPPOSITE Score for the 'Gossiping Fox Trot' by Herman Darewski, advertising the *Daily Sketch* competition and prize, c.1921.

ABOVE Step notation for the 'Slow Fox-Trot', from *How to Dance* by Pat Sykes, 1934.

Arthur Murray Dance Studios franchise has 270 studios in twenty-one countries around the world.

I have a great admiration for those who have learnt dance steps from dance manuals. I think it takes a great deal of patience and ambition to work out the footsteps, dots and dashes. Fortunately I came from a time of VHS tapes, then digitisation and screen-based movement from which to learn dance steps, choreography and archived dance works. Learning from a dance manual is akin to putting together a table or shelves from a very famous Swedish furniture store: you will get there in the end, but you will take twice as long as other people and will no doubt have a frustrating experience. That said,

keeping a record of dance is important to human history, so I am grateful for the legacy of written and illustrated dance manuals.

Of course some authors of dance manuals had motivations beyond instructing the public and leaving a record for posterity. With Vernon and Irene Castle it was as much about enhancing their brand as it was about education. For Victor Silvester in the first half of the twentieth century and before him Cecil Sharp (1859-1924),[55] who was known for documenting Morris dancing and British country dancing, it was as much about shaping society as it was about helping people to dance. Both took on the role of editor, producer and director of what was right for the British dancing public. Aside from those who just wanted to dance, the foxtrot attracted the attention of those who sought to control public dancing and ensure it was done in the proper way, such as Silvester. In many ways this conflict between escapism and control is what dictates the history of dance and the way in which, when dance styles become popular, often those who undermine new dances eventually try to impose rules that control how much freedom one can have when dancing.

Another dancing fad of which the foxtrot was part soon followed. Dance marathons began in Britain, but they really took off in the United States. In reality the participants were not so much dancing as slow walking or, at times, hanging on for dear life. Dance marathons were a test of endurance that played out as a form of social Darwinism:

ABOVE Advertisement for Victor Silvester's dance music, from *Let's Dance* by Eric Hancox, 1948.

OPPOSITE Front cover to *Let's Dance* by Eric Hancox, 1948. Featuring 'The waltz and the quickstep: dance steps in easy stages'.

competitions in which the last people standing were the winners. Couples danced in close contact for as long as possible, which could be days or weeks, to win a cash prize and potential fame. To watch couples dancing together, albeit mostly walking, for hours on end did not prove to be the most entertaining of pastimes, so promoters added acts from vaudeville, invited celebrity guests and dramatically narrated the action on the dance floor to keep the audience entertained.

Dance marathons were at their peak in United States as part of the record-breaking fad of the 1920s. Having remained a lucrative mix of leisure and business opportunity throughout the Great Depression and Prohibition, they eventually ceased to attract public interest and numbers dwindled throughout the 1940s. The film *They Shoot Horses, Don't They?* (1969), starring Jane Fonda and based on the book of the same name by Horace McCoy,[56] who had worked at dance marathons as a bouncer, captures their mood and desperation.

The earliest-known record in dance marathons, or endurance dancing, was set in Sunderland, England, on 18 February 1923[57] by two dance teachers, Olie Finnerty and Edgar Van Ollefin, who danced for seven hours without stopping. Little over a month later, in response to their win, Alma Cummings set the first dance marathon

record in the United States, beginning on Saturday 30 March 1923 at 6.57 pm and ending the next day at 9.57 pm: twenty-seven hours of dancing (the usual format in dance marathons was to dance for forty-five minutes then take a fifteen-minute break) at the Audubon Ballroom at 168th Street and Broadway in New York. Cummings foxtrotted, one-stepped and waltzed to victory, wearing out six partners and several pairs of shoes to beat the British record.

The endurance-inspired record-breaking craze in the United States in the 1920s also involved events such as kissing, hand-holding, talking and laughing contests. One of the most famous record setters of the 1920s was Alvin 'Shipwreck' Kelly, a flagpole sitter.[58] In 1927 he sat for seven days, thirteen hours and thirteen minutes on a flagpole on top of a thirteen-storey building in St Louis. Other more notable record setters were aviators Charles A. Lindbergh, who was the first to complete a transatlantic solo flight, and Amelia Earhart, the first female pilot to fly solo across the Atlantic Ocean.

Dance marathons were a dance-floor theatre of melodrama, power and revenge as couples warred and then made up (or not); there were even marriages. Some of these were real, but many involved mock weddings with quick divorces post-marathon to keep the audience enthused and engaged.[59] Dance marathons are often described as the reality

OPPOSITE Frontispiece, titlepage and demonstrations of how to hold your partner, from *How to Become a Good Dancer* by Arthur Murray, 1942.

FOLLOWING PAGES Photograph of marathon dancers, 20 April 1923.

MR. ARTHUR MURRAY AND DANCING PARTNER

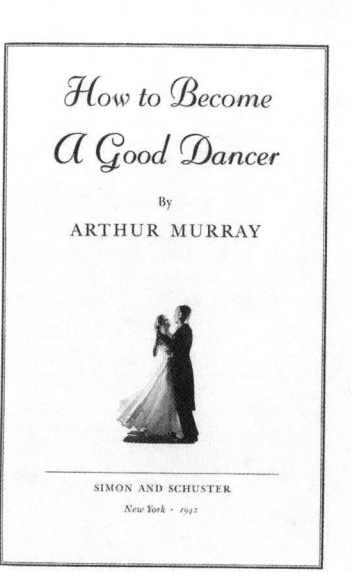

How to Become A Good Dancer

By

ARTHUR MURRAY

SIMON AND SCHUSTER

New York · 1942

HOW NOT TO HOLD YOUR PARTNER

In the photograph above, the girl is not only holding an awkward and unattractive pose, but a very tiring one for her partner.

Shortly after the World War, some of the younger dancers indulged in antics like the pose above. Fortunately, that was twenty years ago.

54

HOW TO HOLD YOUR PARTNER

Both partners should stand comfortably erect, and close enough to one another so that each step is easily followed.

The man's right arm is correctly placed around the girl, with hand held just below her shoulder blade.

55

They've just become engaged, and where there's no sense there's no feeling.

The non-stop baby needs new shoes.

THE DANCING MARATHON

"The first hundred hours are the hardest"

Sketches by Johan Bull

The gentleman seems to have lost the spirit of the thing.

The hours I spend with thee, dear heart, are but a string of blisters.

What a difference just a few hours make! The light fantastic grows a trifle heavy.

The odds are against him.

TV shows of their day, with plots of love, loss and so on about the dancers narrated by a master of ceremonies to squeeze out as much entertainment as possible and keep the audience in their seats. In many ways dance marathons gave a space for those escaping the darkness of the Depression era to forget their troubles and indulge in what was really a crude way to watch people who were more desperate than themselves.

In the United States hundreds of participants and competitions drew audiences in their thousands to dance marathons, which became a regular leisure activity. They offered both financial reward and potential fame to the participants, and it's easy to see that in a time of limited financial options the opportunity of winning a cash prize by dancing with a partner was an enticing prospect. Would-be entertainers and professionals looking to advance their careers shared the dance floor with amateurs hoping only to make some money to get by. Financial gain in turn bred greed, and dodgy

deals by promotors eventually gave the dance marathons a bad reputation.

This dancing world was more about conserving energy than showing off your best dance moves: unenthusiastic foxtrots, slow-paced walks and one steps were the order of the day. However, there was some pizzazz when competitors were given their moment in the spotlight to sing or dance. If the audience members enjoyed the show they would throw coins to the performers. These breaks in the dancing not only increased the entertainment in the long-drawn-out dance marathons, but more importantly they enabled the dancers to earn extra money.

Many a contest left some dancers clinging to their partners, all stamina gone. Floor judges carefully monitored the dancers with a keen eye. The sight of a knee touching the floor meant instant elimination. Gender did not necessarily influence stamina: whether you were male or female, exhaustion could still creep up. Women fared very well in dance marathons, which led to debate on the difference in physical ability between men and women; many men just would not accept that women's physical ability and endurance levels could be greater than their own. Another debate came from reformers who went to dance marathons to save the women from what at times could be degrading events. Prostitution was sometimes arranged at these events, with what were known as 'snake rooms' set aside for financial and sexual exchanges.[60] A clash of working- and middle-class identities sometimes surfaced as the educated middle-class women, who viewed prostitution as degradation, tried to save the working-class women, who saw it as an opportunity for independent earnings and thus survival.

As the 1930s came to a close many states began to ban dance marathons, seeing them as dangerous events, both morally and physically. The growing film industry wanted the dance marathon audiences in its picture houses and made active moves to change legislation and ban the marathons. Dance can be at once both the most beautiful and the oddest thing in the world; the pain and agony of the dancers in dance marathons must have been gruelling, and it's unthinkable that dance marathons on the same scale could ever come back in the twenty-first century.

In many ways you could compare social media to dance marathons: in both cases the incentives to dance include money and potential fame. A short dance clip of a minute or less on social media can raise both revenue and the dancer's profile. Social media could even be seen as the ultimate dance marathon, with that one-minute clip available to watch twenty-four hours a day, almost anywhere in the world.

Dance marathons show the journeys that dance forms can take, whether short-lived crazes or well-established forms with a long lifespan. The foxtrot, like many other dances, exploded into the world; these popular dance trends, fads and crazes were then tested through their staying power on the dance floor.

In the twenty-first century dances like the foxtrot are mostly seen in professional or semi-professional spaces, and often in ballroom performances more akin to dance sport than spontaneous dancing events, though there are exceptions. Social patterns change, music changes and it's the music that leads (or walks hand in hand with) new dance trends. As music evolved – ragtime into jazz, then blues and rock 'n' roll – dances and those who danced them also evolved, taking inspiration from the music to introduce a new and youthful energy to the dance floor. As we take these trips through time it becomes easier to understand how the dance floor and its music have been re-explored from generation to generation and continue to evolve.

OPPOSITE 'The Dancing Marathon: "The first hundred hours are the hardest"' by Johan Bull, from *Judge* magazine, 19 May 1923.

THIS PAGE Photograph of Ann Lawanick holding up her partner Jack Ritof after he has fallen asleep during the marathon dance at the Merry Garden Ballroom in Chicago, 1930.

CHAPTER 05

LATIN NIGHTS

CUBA IS AN island in the north of the Caribbean mostly known for rum, cigars, music, dancing and revolution. The Taíno people, who have South American origins, originally inhabited Cuba until Spanish colonisation in the fifteenth century. The arrival of the Spanish brought disease, wiping out around two-thirds of the indigenous people, who had no natural immunity.[61] More diseases such as measles, along with the harsh realities of colonisation, meant that the Taíno people and their history all but disappeared from mainstream Cuban life. Cuba later gained nominal independence after the American–Spanish War in 1898. A coup in 1959 saw then leader Fulgencio Batista replaced by Fidel Castro, bringing Communist rule to Cuba. Castro defended Cuba from the United States' attempts to remove him from power. Famously a United States-backed local militia, the Democratic Revolutionary Front, planned to invade and overthrow Castro at the Bay of Pigs in 1961, but without success. In October 1962 Castro and Cuba caught the world's attention in a tense thirteen-day military stand-off between the United States and the Soviet Union over the installation of Soviet armed nuclear missiles in Cuba, 90 miles from the United States coast.

Underneath the beauty of Cuba, as with many Caribbean countries, is a history of colonisation, slavery and political change that both scarred and defined the rich culture within it. Much of Cuba's architecture, the worn-out façades of its colonial past, are as much beauty as they are beast. Spanish period architecture sits alongside Neoclassical and Baroque buildings that through time have formed the identity of cities like Havana. They hold within them past glories of old powers and their decaying framework echoes their isolation from capitalism and the industrialised West.

But Cuba also has the rich music and dance culture we know today, such as rumba. Rumba,[62] and what is thought of as 'real' rumba – non-commercial social rumba – is said to have come from the Matanzas Province in Cuba and developed between the 1850s and 1860s. With the abolition of slavery in Cuba in October 1886 Black Cubans had more opportunity to meet to dance and be together. The early days of rumba were an occasion to party and a celebration of music, life and dance where slaves and freed Black people openly drank, danced, cavorted and expressed themselves uninhibitedly. Echoes of past lives and systems of oppression wove Cuban rhythms with those of Haiti and West Africa into rumba. These echoes appeared in dance and music and provided spiritual escape and a place for both slaves and freed slaves to develop community identity in a foreign land. This was a healing process that decoded African memory and mirrored many such gatherings in and around the Americas and the African diaspora.

Rumba developed as both music and dance from Haitian slaves in Cuba.[63] Side-to-side hip movements and quick side steps, erect torsos leaning forward and back – subtle yet strong, rumba is a dance of celebration, African rhythm, spirituality, sexual energy and power. Through organised celebration and spontaneous gatherings Black Cubans played out an open game of courtship and intent where one might see the male thrust his hips at the female in a move called the *vacunao*, whereby the dance intertwines itself with sexual intention. The action and intention of *vacunao* isn't so difficult to understand, although it would have been seen as exotic, unfamiliar or possibly vulgar through a coloniser's gaze.

In rumba the woman is not submissive; she is empowered, responding with dismissive or humiliating gestures towards the male. It's a game of male and female sexuality that, if the male were to lose, might see him taunted by his peers, but in which humiliation is a risk worth taking. In many ways the *vacunao*

reveals the energy within rumba and its now secular nature – in which dancers can be openly sensual – as Black Cubans become distant from African spiritual and religious practice and move towards rhythmic sensuality – and along with this comes fun, competitiveness and courtship.

During the 1920s and 1930s rumba spread and was transformed in ballrooms all over the world with dancers given a smart suit or tails to distract from its sensuous nature. Films such as *Rumba* (1935), which starred George Raft and Carole Lombard in a story of seduction and gangsters, featured a refined style of rumba: the sophisticated glamour of Raft and Lombard, aimed at the white commercial gaze, was balanced against a backdrop of elaborate folk costumes and puffed and frilly-armed Cuban rumba dancers, who were perceived by their

THIS PAGE 'Negro Dance on a Cuban Plantation', from *Harper's Weekly*, 29 January 1859.

audiences as exotic. European dance floors, waiting and ready for the next big thing, embraced rumba and gave it their own sense of charm, style and sexiness. After the Cuban Revolution in 1959 Cuba redefined itself and rumba was further stitched into the culture, becoming Cuba's national dance. This state-approved symbolism of rumba was transported around the world on a journey that saw Cuban traditional rumba evolve into a new version: rhumba (note the spelling difference).

Rhumba, which is associated with competitive ballroom dancing and dance sport, was the result of a transition from traditional to commercial. It's a Westernised version of Cuban rumba that came to be seen as a more international and marketable style. Rumba was no longer only practised at spontaneous dancing events, parties or clubs; it was remodelled outside Cuba in dance studios and recoded as rhumba, along with official accreditation and what were considered proper competition costumes, adding a sexy layer of glitter and machismo to the dancers. Competitive ballroom dance absorbed Latin dance and European dances to create modern ballroom, encasing histories of dancing bodies, styles and form under glitter balls and bright lights around the globe.

Other dances from Cuba such as mambo, cha cha cha and salsa were also popularised away from their dancing roots. Mambo is both the music – a fusion of swing and Cuban music – and the dance. Developed in Cuba in the 1940s, it was popularised by the Cuban musician Pérez Prado (1916–1989), who was known as the king of mambo. He introduced mambo to an enthusiastic crowd at the Tropicana nightclub in Havana in 1943. This expressive Black Cuban dance emerged alongside *danzon*, a similar dance from Mexico. *Danzon* is a group dance that has its roots in rural English country dancing in the seventeenth century and found its way to France and Spain. Through colonialism and slavery it arrived in Mexico and later in Cuba, where it mixed with African and Afro-Cuban dances and became a slow syncopated partner dance. Developing in parallel with this was mambo, which mixes rock steps, side steps, kicks, turns and staccato movements and is as much about feeling the music as it is about perfecting the steps.

Cha cha cha was danced to the music of the same name, notably that written by the

OPPOSITE Score for 'La Rumba', 1912.

THIS PAGE 'Rhumba Lesson No. 2: "The Forward and Backward Step"' by Paul Shahin with Dick Salle and his Society Orchestra, Vogue Picture Record R738. Part of the box set *Learn to Dance the Rhumba (Beginners)*, 1946.

OPPOSITE Poster for the film *Rumba*, starring George Raft and Carole Lombard, 1935.

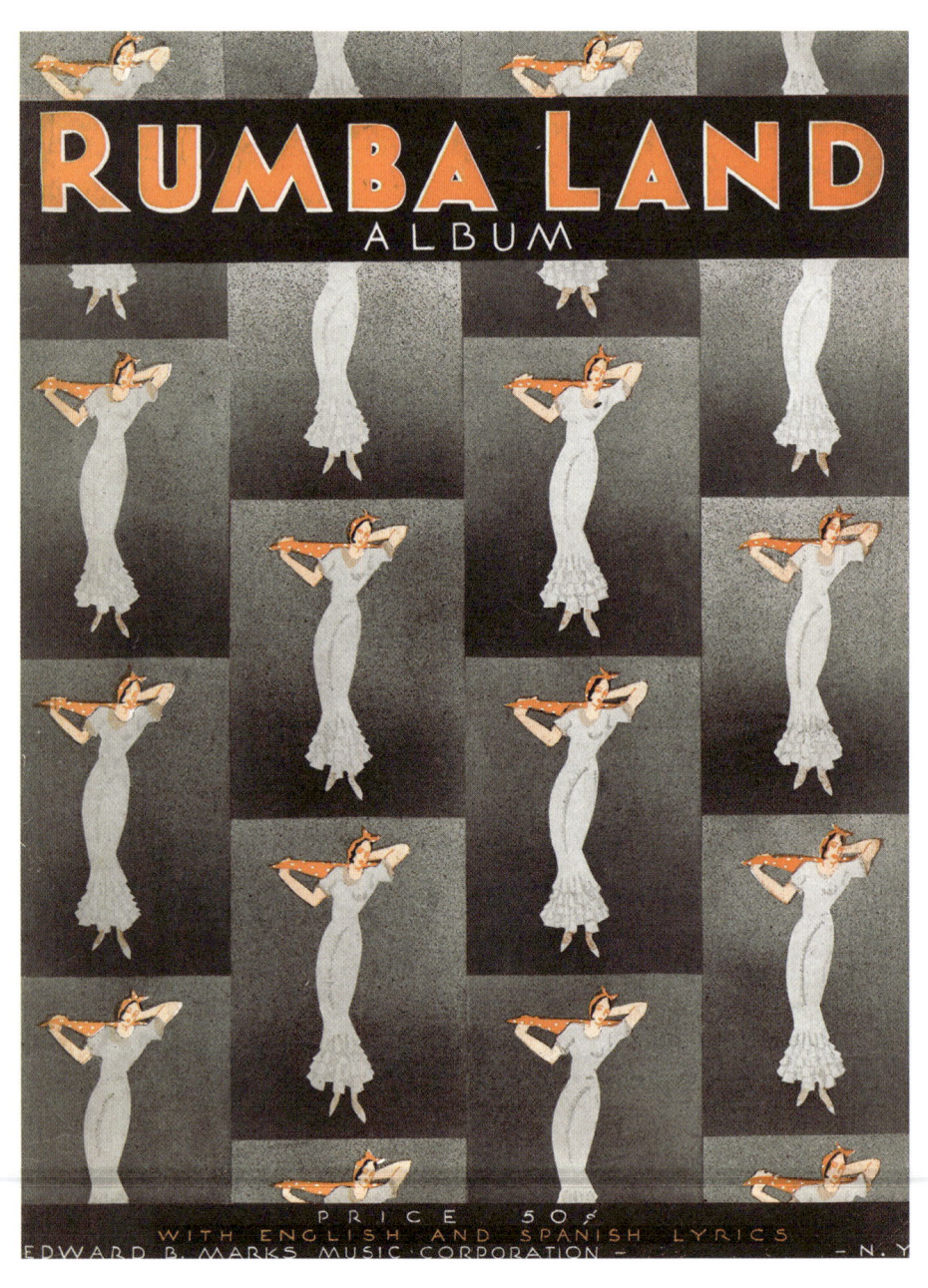

ABOVE Front cover to the songbook *Rumba Land Album*, 1932.

DANCING IN TIME • LATIN NIGHTS

ABOVE (top left) Front cover to publicity brochure for the Tropicana nightclub in Havana, Cuba, 1950s. (top right) Advertisement for the Cuban musician Senén Suárez performing at the Tropicana nightclub. Printed on front: 'Conjunto Senen Suarez. Cuban Rhumba Band Featured Daily at Tropicana. "A Paradise Under the Stars"'. (bottom) Photograph of Carmen Miranda performing at the Tropicana nightclub by Vincent Muñiz, 8 July 1955.

DANCING IN TIME • LATIN NIGHTS

Cuban composer Enrique Jorrín (1926–1987), in the early 1950s. An Afro-Cuban partner dance – hands held or apart, with small dance steps forward and back with swaying hips – that is danced socially, cha cha cha is counted as two slow beats followed by a syncopated 'cha cha cha', though there are variations in the counting in ballroom and competitive cha cha cha. Similar foot patterns can be found in Afro-Cuban dances related to the Santería religion in Cuba.

Salsa followed, originating in Cuba at the end of the nineteenth century with roots in Afro-Cuban rumba and *danzon*. It evolved and shifted through the Caribbean islands, notably in Puerto Rico and Dominica, before being taken to New York, where it was popularised. A partner dance in which the movement rotates in a figure of eight with prominent hip movements, with footwork requiring quick changes of direction, turns, spins and constant weight transitions, salsa has many variations in style and name – including LA-style, casino and New York-style – as well as being familiar in competitive ballroom dancing. Salsa has fluctuated a great deal in popularity; it famously featured in *Dirty Dancing* (1987) starring Patrick Swayze and Jennifer Grey. Unlike dance fads such as the twist, which are immensely popular and then fade away as the next dance comes along, salsa and many similar

Latin dances remain popular because of the steady enthusiastic devotees to salsa who regularly attend local social venues.

Yet through migration Latin dances like rumba exist both at home in Cuba and around the world. Mambo, salsa, cha cha cha and rumba can be found in the United States and many other places around the world where Cuban-born people have migrated, carrying with them the memory of home and their ancestors. They have set up homes and communities in places like Miami and continue to dance traditional rumba, far removed from competitive ballroom rhumba with its glitterballs, costumes, fake tans and bright lights. Many if not all of the dances in this book have migratory stories of transformation; they are developed through tradition, misunderstandings or misinterpretation and even misspellings. Dances change through time and sometimes, as in the case of rumba and rhumba, they are reinterpreted and become something else entirely.

One obvious difference between rumba and rhumba lies in the nature of their performance and their dress codes. Rhumba calls for enhanced and hyper-magnified sexiness and costuming, swapping the everyday dress of working Cubans dancing

OPPOSITE Poster for the film *Cha-Cha-Cha Boom!* featuring Pérez Prado, 1956.

These dances have many different styles and finding the right one for you can be difficult, but it is rewarding when you do. Dance is a magnet, sometimes even a burden, for those of us who cannot escape that tune or the moment that calls us to merge our physical and spiritual selves with the music. Perhaps if I had grown up in Cuba I would have had a completely different relationship with dance – it would have been wired into my everyday experience, and self-expression through dance would have been expected. Instead my initial exposure to dance was in the north of England in the 1970s, where dance did not fit with the narrative of masculinity. Luckily hip hop appeared, along with great music and nightclubs, and dance became all that mattered to me.

rumba for shimmery dresses and open-necked shirts, pronounced chests and a demonstration of a heterosexual dreamscape of heightened masculinity and femininity. Ironically there are many gay people who are dominant in the competitive dance sport scene[64] and who challenge old narratives of masculinity in this space, presenting a camp or ambiguous masculinity when dancing. The boxer Nicola Adams and her partner Katya Jones appearing as same-sex partners on *Strictly Come Dancing* in the UK in 2020, followed by the baker John Whaite and his partner Johannes Radebe in 2021, were landmark moments in sexuality and gender equality, prompting a refreshingly open discussion and, hopefully, inspiring future opportunities for diversity both in the media and on the dance floor.

When choosing between the rhumba and rumba, my advice is to follow the music.

Crossing the water from Cuba to Brazil we are once again presented with some of the most extraordinary rhythmical sounds and dances. Samba is widely thought to have descended from *batuque*, a circle dance that has origins in Angola and what was the kingdom of Kongo,[65] combined with a mix of cultural and religious practices from both the West African Yoruba religion and Catholicism. It is a dance of beautifully textured rhythms, hips and pulsating beats often identified with Rio de Janeiro and Carnival. Brazil was one of the last places to abolish slavery, in 1888. As slavery ended rural commerce was edged away into urban industry and migration to cities abounded.

ABOVE Photograph of a samba group in Rio de Janeiro, 1940s.

OPPOSITE Score for 'Castle Maxixe' by James Reese Europe and Ford T. Dabney, 1914.

Ex-slaves hoping for a better life travelled to the city in search of new opportunities and developed communities of their own. Rio became a central destination for wandering Black Brazilians, one where music and dance slowly formed into samba.

Another dance which is thought to have been instrumental in the development of samba is *candombe* (see page 62), a slave dance from Uruguay which takes on the spirits of the *orishas*. The dancer then assumes different characters, each with personalised rhythms and movement. For example undulating shoulders evoke a sea god, or stamping of the feet the god of war. One of the gods from the *orishas*, *caboclo*, has a style known as the samba. The samba we now know is a secular version of *candombe* and has become a symbol of Brazilian identity and expression.[66]

I have been fortunate enough to travel to Brazil and visit both Rio and São Paulo, two incredibly beautiful places. São Paulo is a very densely populated city with the most inspiring street art on a mass scale. Rio and Copacabana Beach are picture-perfect. When you look up in the evening, as the bright dots of streetlights and lights from windows in the *favelas* (the slums) illuminate the skyline, you begin to understand that you are in a place of extremes. The streets of London can change from the loveliest well-kept Victorian houses to a tired-looking council estate in the blink of an eye, but this is something different.

The gulf between rich and poor in Brazil is plain to see and the varying skin tones of Black people in Brazil are an obvious legacy of its involvement with slavery. Racial mixing, which is very much part of Brazil, is evident and reflects extremely complicated day-to-day social inequalities, weaving a temporal value system that marks a part of Brazil's national identity. The mixed skin tones likewise reflect the heart of samba's evolution as European dances mixed with distant African memory and rhythms. From the twentieth century European social events in Brazil looked back to those of their home continent, with waltzes, polkas, quadrilles and maxixes. As time went by African rhythms and dances became more appealing to the Europeans living in Brazil.

Maxixe from Rio de Janeiro developed around the mid- to late nineteenth century and is sometimes called the Brazilian tango.[67] It is a dance of close embrace, which like the tango or rumba can suggest the intention of sexual advances towards one's

partner through body-to-body movements, sometimes described as a grinding motion of bodies and interlacing legs. The maxixe's influences include European waltz and polka, Afro-Latino social dances such as the *milonga* and *danzon*, and *lundo*, which originated with the Bantu people of sub-Saharan Africa, who arrived in Brazil as slaves brought over by the Portuguese.

No doubt dancing a waltz in a beautiful but wintry ballroom in Bath, England, for example must have been quite different from dancing a waltz in a candlelit garden in Rio. In many ways the merging of European and African expressive cultures such as music and dance seems quite natural, even practical. That said, what rings throughout the history of dance is that human behaviour is, more often than not, motivated by power and money; some win and some lose. Unfortunately poverty and slavery become part of this history as culture develops.

While I was in Rio Carnival was in preparation and I went to visit what is called a *mangueira*; I would describe it as a rehearsal for Carnival. *The mangueira* took place in a massive sports hall and there were about two thousand people in the building. The sound of the drums was intense and the dancing was incredible. As I stood in the middle of the room it was if I was cocooned in a beautiful wall of sound. Watching the dancers holding the rhythms in their bodies made it clear why such a spirited culture is so popular.

There is the undeniable sensuality of the dancers, which is jaw-dropping, and I was stopped in my tracks on more than one occasion by the beauty of some of the dancers. But beyond that, samba is about the legacy of Brazil's past and its rich yet complicated cultural beauty. Experiencing samba culture at that level was incredibly special. My experience, knowing I was an outsider, was momentarily one of both participant and observer.

Samba schools formed in the early part of the twentieth century and were initially scorned by the authorities. The schools competed against each other in *sambadrome* parades. This endures as the most popular

LEFT Photograph of dancers from samba schools in Rio de Janeiro, October 1946.

OPPOSITE Photograph of a samba school parade in the Sambodromo in Rio de Janeiro, 9 February 2013.

image of samba: long stretches of road are marked out, with thousands of spectators on either side watching samba dancers and musicians compete in a mass parade of elaborate costumes and floats.

The spirited nature of samba rings throughout African diaspora dances. Samba is celebratory and closely related to the spectacle of Carnival. In the Georgia Sea Islands off the North Carolina and Florida coastlines in the United States, African slaves developed a Creole language and African-influenced culture known as Gullah.[68] Gullah people lived and worked in the plantations in relative isolation as the environment was too harsh for their masters to stay for extended periods. The slaves on the plantations around the Georgia Sea Islands had more autonomy than many in their position in the United States and they are an example of how African heritage was understood differently across North America, South America and the Caribbean.

African memory was visible in the Gullah people's daily lives, song, food and dance. Dances of ritual and celebration such as the ring shout – a ceremonial dance involving singing, dancing, drumming and clapping[69] – developed more openly than in other slave areas in the United States. The ring shout is a spiritual tradition carried from West Africa and practised by African Americans; its rhythms breathed their way into ragtime and jazz both in music and dance.

In North America, African American expressive culture developed as jazz and hip hop. In South America and Afro-Latino countries such as Brazil it developed as samba along with Caribbean dances such as Cuban rumba. These have more of a spiritual relationship with the *orishas*, an African spiritual practice which comes from the Yoruba[70] people of Congo, Nigeria and surrounding areas of West Africa. Spiritual practices entwined with dances such as the ring shout through the traumatic experience of slavery and developed into rich cultural identities.

CHAPTER 06.

THE CHARLESTON

THE CHARLESTON WAS introduced to the American stage in 1923 in the Broadway show *Runnin' Wild*[71] and comes from African American social dance tradition. Its exact roots before *Runnin' Wild* are hard to define. It's said that the Whitman Sisters (active 1900–43), a famous Black variety act, were already dancing the Charleston in 1911. Another story is that the American entertainer, actor, producer and playwright Flournoy Miller (1885–1971), while on his way to rehearsals for *Runnin' Wild*, saw three young street dancers busking for money outside the Lincoln Theatre with an improvised dance-off to the sound of percussion on garbage cans and kitchen tubs. The lead dancer of the boys was a Russell Brown, who would later become part of the Three Browns, an acrobatic tap troupe. Russell Brown was nicknamed 'Charleston' and he and the other boys often danced steps known as 'Geechie dance'

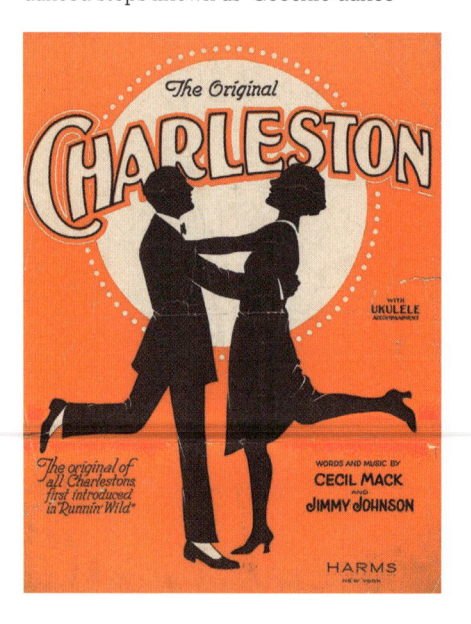

The Original CHARLESTON

WITH UKULELE ACCOMPANIMENT

The original of all Charlestons first introduced in 'Runnin' Wild'

WORDS AND MUSIC BY
CECIL MACK
AND
JIMMY JOHNSON

HARMS
NEW YORK

(another term for Gullah, see page 109), which is said to be similar to the Charleston. This may suggest how the name of the Charleston came about.[72] Miller liked the boys' dancing so much that he asked them to share their steps in rehearsals for the show.

The Charleston went on to take the world by storm in the 1920s. The composer James P. Johnson wrote a song entitled 'The Charleston' that became a big hit for the show. You may be familiar with the catchy piano version through films such as *The Great Gatsby* (2013); it has long been engrained in popular culture. Every time I say 'the Charleston' the tune appears in my head. It's a very memorable song, full of rhythm and a vibrant energy. The Charleston is not the most complicated of dances but, as we can see in photographs and illustrations of the period, it is all about style: a full-bodied rhythmic dance that oozes character, head to shoulders, torso, knees, feet and everything in between.

The black bottom, a dance from the Black rural South of the United States (New Orleans is sometimes mentioned as its

LEFT 'The Original Charleston: With Ukulele Accompaniment. The original of all Charlestons first introduced in *Runnin' Wild*', words and music by Cecil Mack and Jimmy Johnson, c.1923.

OPPOSITE Sheet music for 'Charleston' from *Runnin' Wild*, 1923.

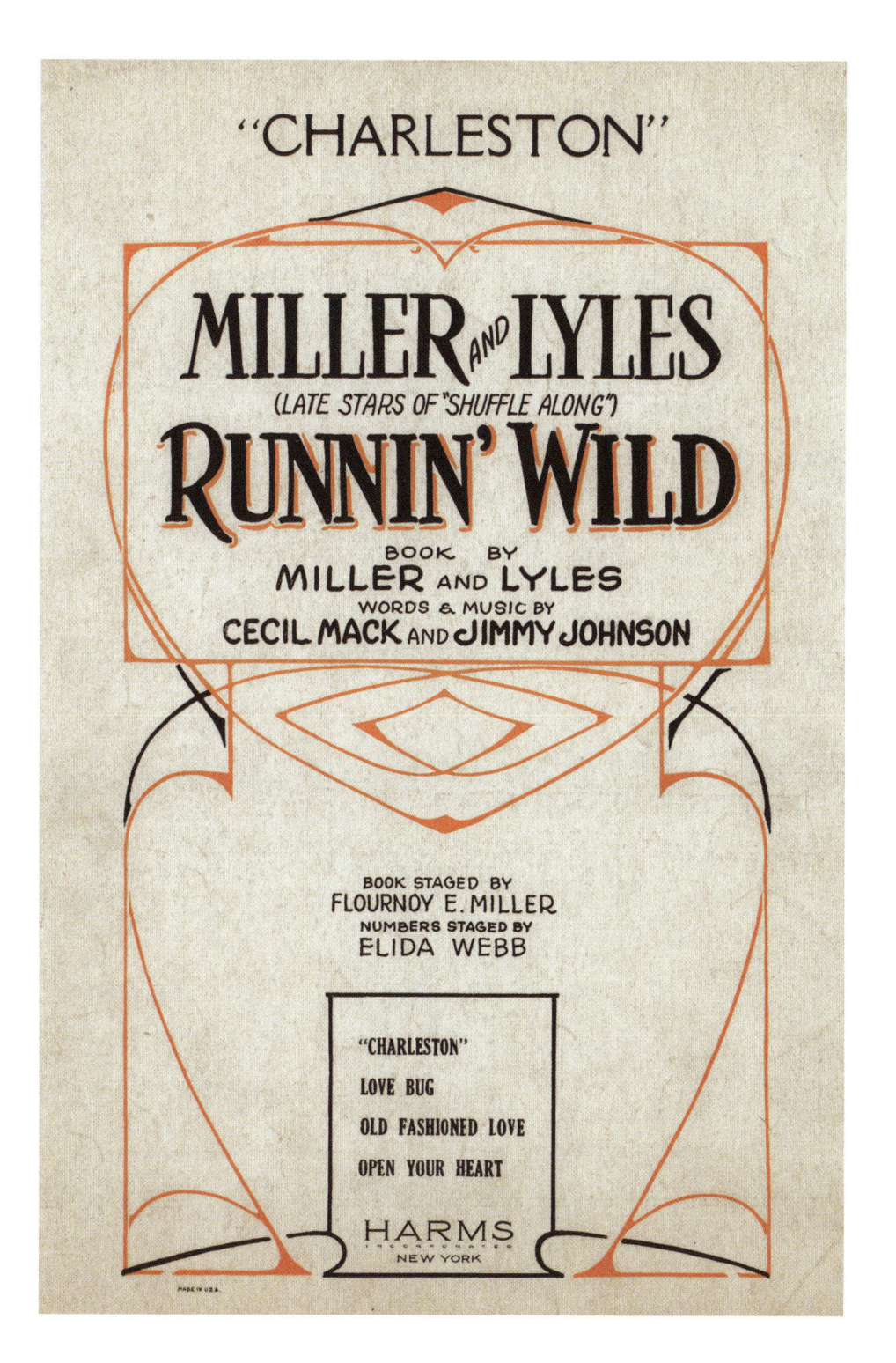

birthplace) arrived on the dance floor shortly after the Charleston. The name black bottom is thought to be taken from an area in Detroit, Michigan. As with many social dances of this time it's difficult to pinpoint exact origins. A solo or partner dance seen as daring, it was danced with a side-to-side or swaying two-step motion. The jazz pianist and composer Jelly Roll Morton (1890–1941) increased the black bottom's popularity by releasing a song in 1925 entitled 'The Black Bottomed Stomp', later called 'The Black Bottom Stomp'. The black bottom, like the Charleston, embedded itself in the Roaring Twenties and the Jazz Age to become a mainstream dance and add to the canon of dance crazes in the early twentieth century.

It is also worth mentioning another dance from this period, the Big Apple, which is thought to have roots in the Gullah ring shout (see page 109) and in square dancing. The Big Apple followed on from the Charleston and was absorbed into the Lindy hop (see page 132). It is a group circle dance in the centre of which sometimes a solo or partner dance appears. The Big Apple was popularised around 1936 at the Big Apple Night Club, from which it took its name – an abandoned African American church, originally a synagogue, in Palmetto, Columbia, South Carolina. The dance is hosted by a 'caller', a master of ceremonies who shouts out the names of popular dances of the day, such as the Susy-Q or Charleston, which are danced either as a whole unit in a big circle or with a solo dancer or couple dancing set pieces or improvisation in the centre of the circle while the other dancers clap or stomp in support to increase the energy.

In the Susy-Q – the origins of whose name are uncertain – the arms are stretched out in line with the centre of the chest with both hands clasped together. The right foot steps over the left leg, which twists and makes a small step that travels to the left; this can be repeated either side. In 1936 Lil Hardin

ABOVE Photograph of Elisabeth Welch and the chorus of *Runnin' Wild*, 1921.

OPPOSITE Musical score for 'Deep River: Black Bottom, New Dance', words by Clifford Seyler, music by Vivian Ellis, c.1927.

FOLLOWING PAGES Musical score for 'Deep River: Black Bottom, New Dance', instructions for the dance by E. Scott Atkinson.

DEEP RIVER

WORDS BY
CLIFFORD SEYLER.
MUSIC BY
VIVIAN ELLIS.

BLACK BOTTOM
New Dance

HOW TO
DANCE
"THE BLACK BOTTOM"
(THE NEW BALLROOM VERSION TAUGHT at the EMPRESS ROOMS)

By

E. SCOTT ATKINSON.

World's Professional Tango Champion, 1925, member
of the famous Instruction Staff of the EMPRESS ROOMS,
Royal Palace Hotel, Kensington, London, W.
Mr SCOTT ATKINSON is photographed here with
Miss DOROTHY COLE World's Tango Champion, 1925,
also of the Empress Rooms.

All Photographs
by HANA.

FULL DESCRIPTION
WITH PHOTOGRAPHS INSIDE

FRANCIS, DAY & HUNTER LTD.,
138-140, CHARING CROSS ROAD, LONDON, W.C. 2.
NEW YORK: LEO FEIST, Inc., 231-5, WEST 40TH STREET
SYDNEY: J. ALBERT & SON, 137-139, KING STREET.
PUBLICATIONS FRANCIS-DAY Société Anonyme, 30, Rue de L'Echiquier, PARIS.

PRINTED IN ENGLAND

2/-
NET.

8   7   6   5

READ F

Back to the left side again	This is a rocking movement from left to right, with a slight "give" with both knees	This completes the half circle with the left leg, which then takes the weight of the body and is a pace from the right	Gentlema left leg "dragge round bel the righ

This leaves you free to start the walk again.   The whole of th

(The Ballroom Version of "Black Bottom

HE FLICK

4	3	2	I
TO LEFT			
entleman's ight foot ushed half a ace to the left, aking the eight of the body	Gentleman's left leg is "dragged" round behind the right and takes the weight of the body	Gentleman's right leg straightens and takes the weight of the body as left knee bends	Gentleman's left leg straight, right knee bent, feet apart

upies 2½ bars, a bar being spent in the drag from Nos. 4 to 6.

e EMPRESS ROOMS, LONDON, W. 8.)

How the Charleston was " Tamed "

These photographs of Mr. E. Scott Atkinson and Miss Dorothy Cole were published in November, 1926. The three top positions show the walk, the side step, and the kick of the " new " Charleston, then approved in all ballrooms. The three positions below are of the equivalent steps in the " old " Charleston, and show clearly why it was banned in many dance centres.

Armstrong (1898–1971), the jazz pianist, composer, bandleader and second wife of the famed jazz trumpeter and composer Louis Armstrong (1901–1971), released a song entitled 'Doin' the Suzie Q' which further heightened its popularity on the dance floor.

The Charleston arrived in Britain in 1925 and kept the dance floors of the early twentieth century very busy. Much like the twist decades later it swept across the world to revitalise dance-floor taste and bring a new energy. Perhaps that is because neither the Charleston nor the twist are the most difficult dances to learn – a twist here, a twist there, or a couple of steps forward and a couple of steps back – unlike the much more complex Lindy hop. The Charleston was a dance for people of all abilities; enthused dancers literally took to the streets in their quest to master it. Victor Silvester commented that people were practising the Charleston in bus queues and tube stations, while waiting for trains or on street corners. Even on-duty police were seen practising the must-have dance steps of the time.[73] (I must admit I have been known to practise dance moves myself when waiting for a bus or while in a queue – not elaborate or even noticeable moves, but I can relate.)

The Charleston represented modernity and a new youthful energy. It was a novel and exciting dance that the flappers could call their own. The dancing energy of these rebellious young women symbolised a changing world and a developing new century of technical innovation, such as the mass production of cars, along with the growth of the women's suffrage movement and the shift towards women's voting rights in Britain in 1918. This was a changing world and it had Charleston and jazz music as its soundtrack. The flappers with their short hair, knee-length dresses and headbands would become one of the strongest images of the Charleston and the Roaring Twenties. The silhouette of the flapper dress, known as *la garçonne*, was said to be based on a boyish, youthful figure, which was a desired look of the time. With this in mind fashion and dress design began to change to suit the new look, with a looser waistline that dropped below the hips and was very different from the flamboyant, fitted dresses of the past.

The Charleston and later the twist brought simple dance steps with maximum fun. The Charleston was both a partner and solo dance, adding space for individual flair and personalised energy in the music. Its syncopations created a different sense of bodily rhythm, a sense that past dances such as the waltz did not have. The Charleston was less rigid than earlier dances and called

OPPOSITE 'How the Charleston was "Tamed"', *Dancing Times*, November 1939.

for expressive interpretation and a freer social climate: a dance craze that asked for an explosive raw attitude and street cool while at the same time facing the challenge of expectations of properness for the English dance floor.

The Charleston's biggest and most spectacular event in Britain was on 15 December 1926, when the theatre impresario C. B. Cochran organised a 'Charleston Ball' at the Royal Albert Hall attended by close to ten thousand people and judged by, among others, Fred Astaire.[74] As with many fads not only did such a large-scale event mark the rise of a fashionable dance form, but it also marked its fall: the Charleston began to decline in popularity some months later. Even at the height of its popularity the dance had its critics and was perceived to be a dangerous threat to the young. Dancing masters such as Victor Silvester,[75] who led one of the biggest-selling dance orchestras at the time and whose music was recorded and popularised by Parlophone, set out to tame the Charleston.

Silvester, a fixture in dance competitions, radio broadcasts and publications such as *Modern Ballroom Dancing* (1927), played a key role in the codification of ballroom dancing and in the Imperial Society of Teachers of Dancing (ISTD). He was a gate-keeper of what constituted proper dance in the UK and a fervent advocate for the English style of dance, often taking 'rough' dances coming from the United States, such as the Charleston, and (as he saw it) refining them to suit what he considered correct form for the British ballroom.

Santos Casani (1893–1983), an actor and ballroom dance teacher, and his dancing partner Jose Lennard went as far as reinterpreting the Charleston as a flat-foot dance,[76] taking out the high-kicking legs, wild arms, low-slung body and elevated levels of energy they saw as primitive to produce what they viewed as a more civilised version for British ballrooms and dance halls. They even showcased the flat-foot Charleston by dancing on the top of a taxi driving through Central London to demonstrate its steadiness and ease with their more gentle approach.[77] Santos Casani also promoted the flat-foot Charleston further through the release of a song-and-dance instructional for the flat-foot version entitled *Casani's 'Come and Do the Charleston'*.[78] The address of the Casani School of Dancing, 90 Regent Street, London – in an area where properties have always commanded high rents – shows how seriously dances like the Charleston were taken at the time.

Casani and Lennard's postures are both upright and the images of them suggest quite small steps forward and back and indicate a

gentle approach to the Charleston that suits an English style. It would have been viewed as a much calmer, more gentrified version of the Charleston than the African American one, and would suit the social position of the British middle and upper classes at the time. There are striking differences between Casani and Lennard's (and Josephine Baker's) interpretation of the Charleston and the African American, more street/club style of the dance.

Josephine Baker (1906–1975) was one of the most well-known dancers of the Charleston. The American-born Baker was to spend much of her professional life in Paris. Born in St Louis, she lived part of her early life in the slums of the city, where she turned to street-corner dancing to make money. She was married twice by the age of 15 and, at the age of 19 and now divorced for the second time, travelled to Harlem in New York to seek opportunities as an entertainer and found herself in the centre of the Harlem Renaissance. Harlem had witnessed an explosion of Black performance in the middle of a still-racist New York. Baker was an artist of great comic wit and sensational dancing skills and soon got the attention she wanted, going on to dance in many shows, such as the groundbreaking Black revue *Shuffle Along* (1921).[79]

Josephine Baker had a tumultuous relationship with her mother from an early age. Even after she had achieved fame and enough money to look after her mother and half-sister, financially things were difficult. Baker's relationship with her mother and the racism in America eventually pushed her to move to France.[80] On 2 October 1925 Baker found herself at the Théâtre des Champs-Élysées in *La Revue Negre* in Paris. André Daven, the owner of the theatre, was initially disappointed with the show, complaining that there was too much tap dance and that the gospel music did not meet his requirements. He asked Jacques Charles, a choreographer from the Moulin Rouge, to rework the show and the two decided that Baker was more suited to the less inhibiting Charleston rhythms, which in turn would no doubt have been more alluring to a Parisian audience.

This is when Baker's routine 'Danse Sauvage' (wild dance) was developed. It was a duet with Joe Alex, who would wear a feather-covered loin cloth. Charles wanted Baker to appear on stage topless, wearing only a satin bikini covered in pink flamingo feathers. At first Baker protested and expressed a desire to return to the United States, but she was

OPPOSITE Sheet music for 'Casani's "Come and Do the Charleston": The New Flat Charleston', words by Clifford Seyler, music by Vivian Ellis, c.1927.

convinced to perform the first show, which initially received mixed reactions from the audience.[81] Baker would grow into her new role, however: Paris adored her and she soon moved on to the Folies Bergère, where she performed her famous banana dance while wearing a string of artificial bananas and little else.[82] Baker's skin tone, perceived negatively in the United States, was celebrated along with her curves and sensuality in France.

Opportunities were as much social as professional, and Josephine Baker often mixed with high society. During the Second World War she was recruited by the Deuxième Bureau, a branch of French military intelligence, to gather information and was later given the title of Honourable Correspondent for her part in the war effort. Her charm and connections in the Parisian social scene gained her access to the most exclusive venues in Paris: she mixed with the elite in embassies and at the most prestigious café-society events, where she specialised in gathering intelligence about German military locations. She later attempted to relaunch her career in the United States but soon learnt that fame did not outweigh the racism still prevalent there, so she returned to France.

However iconic the image of Josephine Baker and the banana dance, I think that it might be misleading as to what and who she really was. There is a clip of Baker on YouTube dancing the Charleston in 1925. Her comic facial expressions are a little distracting but are of their time, and the dancing shows great finesse, rhythm and character. It's interesting to consider how different her dancing might have been off the stage, expressing herself in a space where she did not have to entertain or be 'other' for an audience.

For most dancers, particularly those whose craft is based on improvisational dance, their performance on stage is very different from how they would dance in a jam, party or club. I think there is a lot we are yet to know about dance through these lost moments of dancing genius behind the scenes, away from an audience's eye or a camera lens. The exciting thing is that off-stage footage does turn up every now again in archives, and it shows dancing from a different time and in a different light. As a collector of dance ephemera and film I look forward to stumbling across unseen dancing footage. It enables me to understand a little more about the dancing of a particular time, and often I am blown away by the physicality. Perhaps in the future we may come across some new footage of Josephine Baker or others such as the Nicholas Brothers: film archive that reveals a different side of their dancing away from the stage.

OPPOSITE Photograph of Josephine Baker performing at the Folies Bergère in Paris, France by Walery, c.1926.

Like other dances the Charleston migrated and shifted its way around the world. Following its explosion in the 1920s the Charleston moved a few blocks up into the South Bronx of the early 1980s and become known as the Charlie rock. This version was made famous by Wayne 'Frosty Freeze' Frost (1963–2008) of Rock Steady Crew. Charlie rock is a style of top rock – the standing-up introduction of breaking (often mislabelled as breakdancing) before the dancer goes down to the floor. It's the breaker's introduction to his opponent or to the crowd and is usually a cross step to the left then to the right or vice versa. Top rock has an extensive vocabulary of steps such as the Indian step; some were comical, some were confrontational, but all were funky. Charlie rock has the same foot and leg patterns as the Charleston. Frosty Freeze, like Baker, was known as a strong character dancer (although without the exaggerated facial expressions of dancers of Baker's time).

With its relative ease and focus on style the Charleston made the dance floor a freer and more accessible place. In my opinion even Victor Silvester's intention for the English

version to be subdued and respectable ironically gives the flat-foot Charleston a coolness and character of its own; the stiffness and control of the upper body encapsulate a particular Englishness. The Charleston is in its simplicity a very versatile dance with so much variety, nuance, rhythm and character. This is the reason it reappears throughout time and continues to appeal to a new generation. The Charleston and Josephine Baker are such are a big part of the development of dance and the nature of social dance. Josephine Baker is more than the wiggling hips. For a Black woman to navigate the limited opportunities of the time would have been beyond difficult and Baker's is very much a story of human resilience, strength and determination.

From flapper dresses to the sharp suits of the dancing men, style reigned supreme in the Charleston. Personally I wouldn't say no to occasional plus-fours gracing my legwork; in fact I am sure that such attire enhances the dancing experience. The Charleston reveals the side of you that is usually hidden in your daily life. It's a shake-off, a thing, a get-down. Class, race, gender, age: it doesn't matter. Style is the only thing that does.

OPPOSITE 'The Charleston as Seen at Montmartre', recording the difficulties in mastering the Charleston, by Rose le Quesne, from the *Bystander*, 20 July 1927.

FOLLOWING PAGES Miss Vivian Marinelli giving Charleston dancing lessons to basketball players of the Palace Club, the Washington D.C. entry in the American basketball league. Left to right: Kearns, Manager Kennedy, Conway, woman playing piano, Miss Marinelli, Grody and Saunders. 15 February 1926.

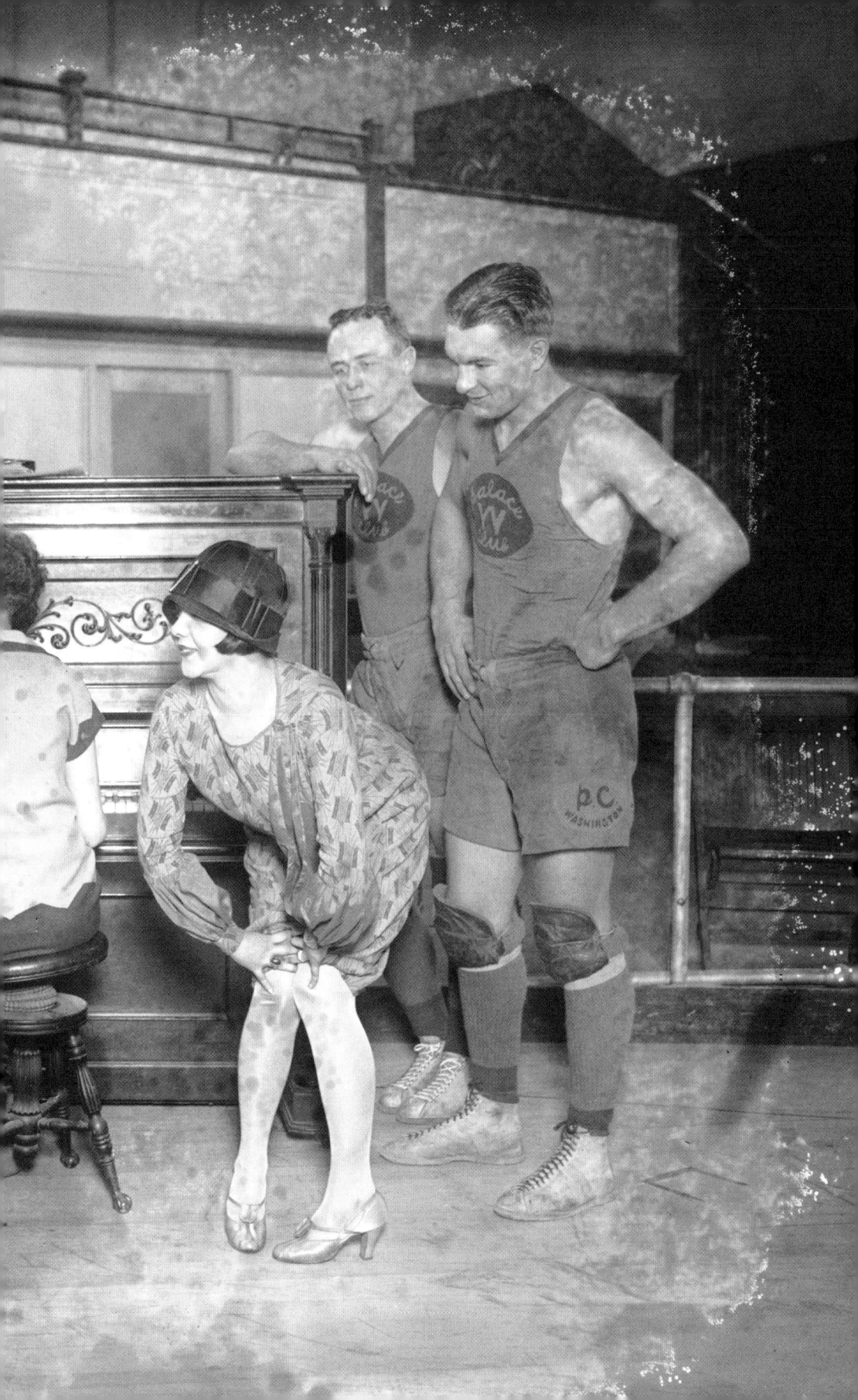

CHAPTER 07.

THE LINDY HOP

THE LINDY HOP grew out of the Savoy Ballroom in Harlem, New York City, around 1927. Originally known as the hop this improvisational partner dance went on to become a popular dance throughout the swing era of the 1930s and early 1940s, spreading from Harlem around the world. The Lindy hop was pioneered by dancers like George 'Shorty' Snowden (1904-1982), also known as Shorty George, at the Savoy. Snowden was in a comedy dance act with his partner Big Bea, who stood at six feet while Snowden was five foot two inches, which must have been a sight to behold. Shorty George and the Shorty George Trio were the first to take the Lindy hop out of the Savoy. The trio was made up of three teams: Shorty George and Big Bea, Leroy Stretch and Little Bea, and brother-and-sister team Madeline and Freddie. They also worked alongside another performer, 'Twist Mouth' Ganaway, who was said to be the best dancer at the Savoy Ballroom; Ganaway performed the Lindy hop but not as part of the Shorty George Trio; instead he chose to perform separately from the group and under his own name.

The name Lindbergh was on everyone's lips in the late 1920s as Charles Lindbergh became the first person to fly solo across the Atlantic from New York to Paris in 1927, making him a household name. He was dubbed 'Lucky Lindy' and his triumphant journey across the Atlantic was greeted with newspaper headlines such as 'Lindy Hops the Atlantic',[83] bringing the term 'hop' with the name 'Lindy' into common use. What we know as the Lindy hop was at first simply called 'the hop' and then for a short while the 'Lindbergh hop'; 'Lindbergh' was most likely added to match the spirit of the time.

The dance we know today became known as the Lindy hop in 1928. George Snowden and his then partner Mattie Purnell entered and won a Charleston dance marathon on 17 June 1928 at the Manhattan Casino, New York.[84] Snowden demonstrated some fancy footwork steps in a breakaway[85] – a short solo when the dancers momentarily separated from one another and which enabled them to showcase their personal repertoire through acrobatics, fancy footwork and general showing off. Snowden was interviewed after the competition by a reporter from Fox Movietone News who asked him the name of the steps. Shorty George was present and replied, 'the Lindy'; and so the hop became the Lindy hop.[86]

A partner dance called the Texas Tommy, including the breakaway, is thought to have been an initial influence on the Lindy hop. With a basic eight-count rhythm, the Texas

OPPOSITE 'The Savoy', lithograph by Dayton Branfield, New York City WPA Art Project, 1935-43.

NEW YORK CITY WPA ART PROJECT   The Savory   Dayton Brandfield

Tommy first appeared in San Francisco in the early part of the twentieth century. The Lindy hop borrowed from such dances as the Texas Tommy and the Charleston, adding its own sense of musicality and self-expression, but giving itself a template on which to grow alongside the evolution of swing music. Taking what were once ragtime steps and adapting them to the music, the Lindy hop demonstrated rhythmic and improvisational virtuosity.

There were other innovators of the Lindy hop, notably Whitey's Lindy Hoppers, who became the most well-known Lindy hop group. Whitey's Lindy Hoppers were named after Herbert 'Whitey' White, an African American former bouncer at the Savoy Ballroom who saw the financial opportunity for the Lindy hop beyond the Savoy and took Whitey's Lindy Hoppers from Harlem into showbiz. Frankie Manning (1914–2009) of Whitey's Lindy Hoppers developed the choreographic potential of the Lindy hop and was also the first to develop air steps – dynamic throws over the shoulders, lifts, catches and bodies flying away then back to each other at breakneck speed.

Manning developed a move known as over-the-back in which his partner Freda Washington was flipped off and over his back.

This was first demonstrated in 1935 at a dance competition at the Savoy Ballroom in which George Snowden famously challenged some of the younger Lindy hoppers.[87] The over-the-back move caused a sensation. Later Snowden asked Manning where he got the move from and Manning replied, 'from you'. Manning had been inspired by one of Snowden's lifts with his partner Big Bea, in which she would lift Snowden onto her back and carry him around.

Air steps and Whitey's Lindy Hoppers were featured in short choreographed pieces, notably in the films *A Day at the Races* (1937) and *Hellzapoppin'* (1942). These captured Lindy hop dancers such as Norma Miller (1919–2019) on screen, swinging, flying, dropping and falling to take partner dancing in a new dynamic, rhythmical and physical direction. Al Minns (1920–1985) and Leon James (1913–1970) from Whitey's Lindy Hoppers also went on to pioneer and develop jazz dance in the 1940s and 1950s.[88] Dancing to jazz at the Savoy preceded studio-based commercial jazz, yet there are still whispers of its motion and movement in modern street dance as we know it today.

From their beginnings up until the Second World War, Whitey's Lindy Hoppers would go from strength to strength. In 1939 eight of the group, led by Frankie Manning, went on a near year-long tour of Australia and

OPPOSITE 'Harlem WPA Street Dance, 1937', lithograph by Elizabeth Olds, New York City WPA Art Project, 1935–43.

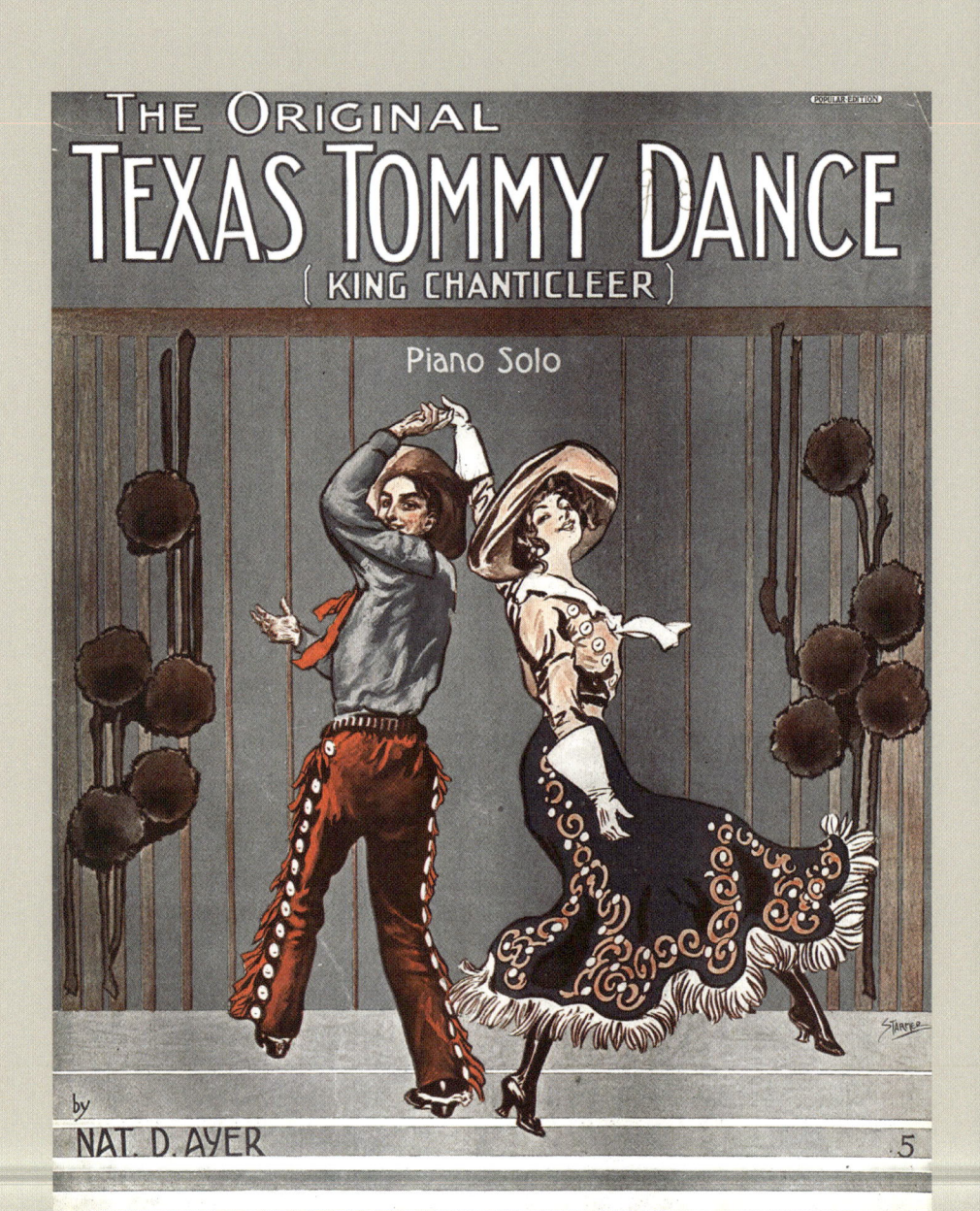

New Zealand. Meanwhile some remaining Lindy Hoppers joined the Broadway show *Knickerbocker Holiday*, as well as appearing at the New York World's Fair. That performance featured as many as forty Lindy Hoppers, who were promoting the Savoy Ballroom and who were billed as 'The Savoy World's Greatest Colored Dancers'.

The show was part of an exhibit showcasing Black cultural art with an all-Black staff, band and cast of performers – albeit the exhibit had a white owner, Moe Gale. The Lindy Hoppers would perform twenty-minute shows up to thirteen times a day from noon to midnight, or sometimes until 2 am. These shows told the story of how jazz dance evolved into the Lindy hop and included an African dance demonstration. That same year the Lindy Hoppers were featured in a swing version of *The Hot Mikado* on Broadway and in a Big Apple Contest.[89] The Big Apple was a formation dance which revealed more of the social spirit of Lindy hop in contrast to the air steps favoured in Hollywood films; it was centred on the joy and togetherness of the dancers and had an energy reminiscent of jazz. This energy was to some extent lost as the Lindy hop's evolution continued into a more performance-orientated version that favoured dancing for an audience over the dancers' dancing for each other.

At the root of jazz is the famed Black American dancer Master Juba (1825–1852),

whose real name is believed to have been William Henry Lane and who danced in London from 1848 to 1852.[90] Juba, once a minstrel dancer, was the forefather of tap. His dance skills were so admired that on his death in 1852 while still in the UK his skeleton was displayed in a music hall in Sheffield[91] (although this claim is not proven) so that people could be amazed at the inner workings of his spectacular dancing body.

Juba was captured in print by Charles Dickens in *American Notes for General Circulation: Volume 1*.[92] On seeing Juba dance in the Five Points area of Manhattan Dickens described him as having 'two right legs, two wooden legs, two wire legs, two spring legs, – all sorts of legs and no legs'.[93] Juba was also famed for his dance challenges in the area, notably against John Diamond (1823–1857), a white dancer whom

OPPOSITE Score for 'The Original Texas Tommy Dance (King Chanticleer)' by Nat D. Ayer, 1913.

ABOVE Photograph of dancing at the Savoy Ballroom in Harlem, New York City, 1947.

he famously beat.[94] There is still a lot to learn and to understand about Juba, not just about his dancing skill, but also about his life in the UK; I hope one day we will discover where in London he lived and danced.

The Savoy Ballroom in Harlem in the 1930s and 1940s was the place to be for dancers; that is dancers of a certain kind, the sort who demanded challenging rhythms, tones and tempos to develop new ways of moving. The majority of the dancers at the Savoy Ballroom were of African descent and much of the music had African roots; however, the Savoy was a racially mixed social space.[95] It was groundbreaking not only in dancing and music but as an inclusive venue where white and Black could mix and where music and dancing were the agenda. Unlike the Cotton Club, which was run on a segregated system with white audiences only, the Savoy ignored the colour-bar policies of the time. Women asking men to dance was still seen as improper until the Second World War, when it was briefly considered respectable in view of women's part in the war effort;[96] this later reverted after the war when gender dynamics largely returned to pre-war norms.

The Lindy hop was an expressive, athletic and competitive dance in which the latest steps of the day were tested, invented, performed and perfected through the improvisational and rhythmic energy of both dancers and musicians. The drummer Chick Webb and his orchestra, the Savoy Ballroom house band, both inspired and were inspired by the Lindy hop dancers. This back and forth encouraged new dance skills and rhythms between the dancers and musicians[97] and mirrored the collaborative development and community joy visible in African traditions such as that of the ring shout (see page 109); unity and creativity were at the core of Savoy dance.

Although the Savoy Ballroom was unsegregated, there were other frictions on the dance floor. Social dance can be unifying but it can also be furiously competitive and territorial. The northeast 141st Street corner of the ballroom to the right of the band shell, known as the cat's corner,[98] where only those at the top of the dancing tree danced, was for the professional Lindy hoppers.[99] It was a sacred place into which the uninitiated wandered at their peril, a space silently reserved for those who thrived, innovated and defended their dancing reputation and a space for dance challenges, either organised or spontaneous, that could cement or end a dancer's rule. Here, showing off and being the best mattered. The Savoy Ballroom housed two bandstands with Chick Webb's orchestra holding court at the cat's

OPPOSITE Photograph of the American Lindy hop dancer Norma Miller and her long-time dance partner, Billy Ricker, in action, Chicago, Illinois, c.1940. Known as the 'Queen of Swing', Miller later formed her own dance troupe; she was also a choreographer, actor, writer and comedian.

corner. The bandstands were used to ensure a continuous flow of music. If one band needed a break the music was blended from one side to the other in a seamless passing of the musical torch. This blending and mixing was later reflected in disco and hip hop and the mixing of one record into another.

The Lindy hop was now out in the wider world for everyone and, like the Charleston and many other social dances before it, it survived its initial introduction into the world as a dance craze and lasted for a few decades in various forms and places;

especially on the west coast of America, where it featured on the big screen in Spike Lee's film *Malcolm X* (1992). Otis Salid choreographed the Lindy hop sections in the film and Frankie Manning was brought in to assist Salid, while Norma Miller was hired to assist Manning.[100]

A change in social dynamics, fashion and musical tastes came about as swing music morphed into bebop during the 1940s and 1950s. Charlie 'Bird' Parker and Dizzy Gillespie were exploring jazz through a faster, unsyncopated pace that did not suit the Lindy hop's tempo and rhythmic flow.[101] Their phrasing was less symmetrical rhythmically and improvised solos were too

ABOVE Photograph of Harlem's Beaux Arts Ball, at which a trombonist regaled the dancing crowd with a hot number at the Savoy Ballroom, New York, March 1942.

OPPOSITE Photograph of African American dancers spending Sunday evening in the Savoy Ballroom in Harlem, New York, February 1956.

DANCING IN TIME · THE LINDY HOP

141

Welcome Home America's
THE KING OF
CHICK
FEATURING THE FIRST LADY OF SWING
ELLA
The Biggest Band
3 GREAT Orchestras
Sunday

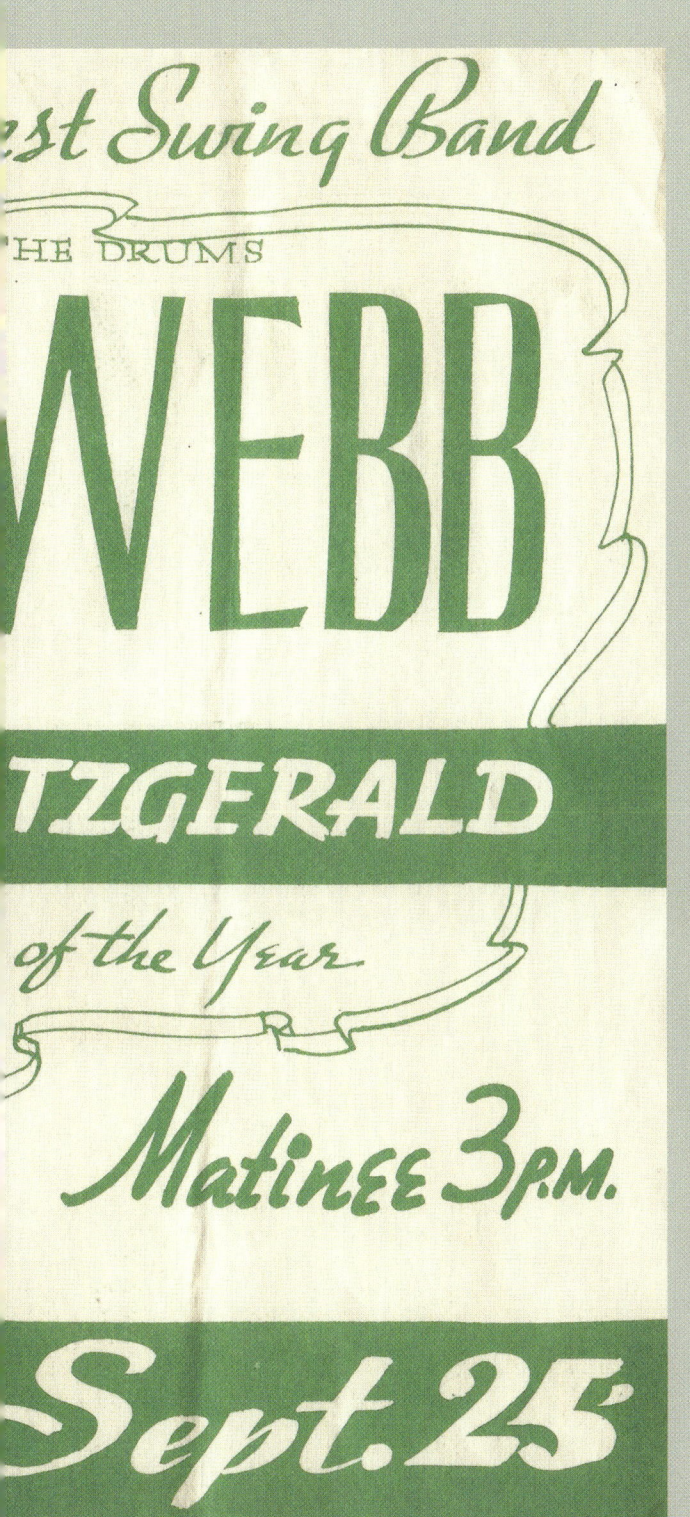

OPPOSITE Advertisement for Chick Webb and Ella Fitzgerald at the Savoy Ballroom, 1938.

unpredictable for the dancers of the time. The leap between syncopated swing and the more radical sound of bebop may also have been simply too sudden a change for the dance floor. The Second World War further broke the momentum of Lindy hop with many of its dancers going to war. After the war Lindy hop had to find itself again and it drifted around the world, taking on different forms and names such as swing, jitterbug[102] and later rock 'n' roll.

Some dances are lost over time; those such as the Lindy hop, which focus on spectacle, are very physical and thus difficult to learn and maintain. Dances with a high level of physicality tend to disappear from mass social dance tastes as dance floors favour gentler, easier steps for mass accessibility. Power changes dramatically in the dance world too; the appeal of dances when introduced into popular culture is fragile, their power only momentary. There are however re-emergences of the Lindy hop, notably in Sweden,[103] where it is seeing its most invigorated revival. In the United States it's a different story: the revival during the 1990s was not under the name of Lindy hop but of swing – a reinterpretation of Lindy hop danced at a slightly slower pace and more formal in its presentation.

One notable name in any discussion of the history of swing and Lindy hop is that of Dean Collins (1917–1984), a white Lindy hopper from Newark, New Jersey. Collins first began learning dance from his sisters at the age of 13. Participation in many amateur dance competitions eventually led him to the Savoy Ballroom, where he saw and learnt the Lindy hop in its heartland. Collins moved to Los Angeles in 1936 and took Savoy-style Lindy hop with him. He began teaching a modified style of the dance which became known as swing and later as West Coast swing or Hollywood-style swing. Collins would go on to make a big impact on Hollywood, choreographing and dancing in films including *Let's Make Music* (1940) starring Bob Crosby, brother of Bing.

West Coast swing was reformatted over time and developed its own approach to the Lindy hop style. One major change was replacing the circular motion in which Lindy hoppers danced together with a slotted format – moving backwards and forwards with your partner instead of working the room in a circle and utilising more of the space. It seems the slotted variation came more from necessity rather than as an intentional deviation from the Lindy hop; dance floors on the West Coast were smaller and the dancers were packed in tightly together; it was all quite a difference from the spaciousness of the Savoy Ballroom. The slotted system worked better and helped dancers avoid being kicked or bumped by other dancers.[104]

The Lindy hop lost its appeal in the mid-twentieth century and for a while was overtaken by other dances. Then on the East Coast of the United States Sandra Cameron, a three-time US Ballroom Champion, reinvigorated the style by first connecting with Al Minns and persuading him to teach at her school, the Sandra Cameron Dance Center, in New York in 1981. Frankie Manning would also teach at the centre six years later.[105] In 1985 the New York Swing Dance Society formed, devoting itself to the revival, preservation and development of swing.[106] The Cat Club was held at an old skating rink on East 13th Street, where people could gather regularly and dance swing. Often dancers such as Frankie Manning would attend, bringing kudos and a sense of tradition to the dance floor.[107]

During this period the different schools of thought about swing such as those on the East Coast and West Coast caused division.[108] The arrival of the internet meant that the infighting within the swing dance community was played out online with different ideas about swing now battling it out both virtually and on the dance floor.[109] Lindy hop struggled as a result and eventually differences between the different camps began to get heated. Given that Lindy hop, like jazz music, played an important part in the development and

history of America, its relative absence on the world dancing scene is surprising. But part of the reason for the lack of visibility of Lindy hop today, aside from the potential difficulty in learning it, may be the separation of Black history, beyond the history of slavery, from mainstream history.

There appear to be pushes to reignite the Lindy hop in the United States and Britain, not just as a popular dance form, but as a legacy of African diaspora culture. I hope that in time the Lindy hop will be re-energised by a new generation. It's not only about rebuilding an inventive dance form, but also about keeping names such as Norma Miller, Frankie Manning, Al Minns, Leon James and many others alive by developing educational opportunities for future generations to understand Lindy hop's legacy and its contribution to African diaspora culture and dance.

More than anything the revival of Lindy hop, especially in the Black community, has the potential to offer catharsis to the African diaspora and support a pride and spirited strength within a community that in many ways continues to be disempowered. This could be a way to celebrate the depth of African culture and the beautiful diversity of its ideas and rhythms.

CHAPTER 08.

DANCE HALLS

MUSIC AND DANCE, dance and music – a match made in heaven, and the dance hall was that heaven. It was a meeting ground for the young, old and in between to find their place on the dance floor, cut a rug, make shapes and have some fun. Dance halls were an extension of the ballrooms of old, but these were places for everyone – working people, the middle and upper classes, and the social elite (though not always in the same venues) – to shake off the modern, increasingly industrial world. They were plush, shiny places with bright lights, fountains, handsome decor and equally handsome people. Dance halls were decorated in optimism, places of wild colour that were a welcome distraction from two world wars.

Dance halls were also an extension of the music halls from earlier decades. Urban industry was growing and towns and cities began to swell with new people looking for work and entertainment. Music halls were developed as social spaces for the working class; pubs, halls and back rooms offered a wide variety of acts including singers, dancers and acrobats. Music halls would also bring in dancers from overseas and American entertainers who introduced minstrelsy and European dance acts such as the waltz and ballet, all of which developed a culture of dance in social spaces that set the stage for dance halls to appear as a new century was ushered in.

Form and properness were of course still the order of the day at the beginning of the twentieth century. But ragtime, jazz, tango, foxtrot, jive, jitterbug and many other dances and musical forms were about to shake up the dance floor. This would test the old guard from the nineteenth century[110] as dance halls transitioned from the relative calmness of the one-step to the leaps, throws and turns of jitterbug. Dance halls thrived from the early part of the twentieth century but faded out in the 1960s as nightclubs and discos made a play for their place in the dancing world. In the 1950s an estimated four million people attended dance halls weekly with an annual audience of around 200 million,[111] which made dance halls the second biggest leisure industry after the cinema.

In Britain dance halls were given an added twist of French decadence and glamour with names such as the Palais de Danse, in Nottingham, or the Palais Royale on

OPPOSITE 'Dancing Couples No. 2' by Anne Harriet Fish, cover design for *Vanity Fair*, March 1921.

Shaftesbury Avenue, London. The names alone of famous dance halls like the Hammersmith Palais captured the desirability of an invitation and a cosmopolitan tone of dancing promise. The Royal Opera House, Covent Garden,[112] both before and throughout the Second World War, was one of the most popular dance halls of the time, as was the Lyceum Theatre in London's Drury Lane. These dance halls were extravagantly decorated, well looked after and, for many patrons, places of great opulence. They were places for both sexes to meet, not just to dance but to socialise. Like many dance venues before them, dance halls were cast in the role of immoral antagonist by the Church.

Dance halls were professionally managed spaces where the working and middle classes could discover themselves, forge new relationships and of course dance. The social elite often attended dance halls with closed membership or private clubs where they were free to party away from prying eyes and an increasingly opportunistic press. Before the First World War most dances were held at community halls or dance schools until the introduction of new metropolitan-type dance halls. The upper and middle classes were the most enthusiastic dancers in this period, having the funds and access to much

more refined venues. They were catered for in music, fashion and appropriate venues that suited their position.

At the upper level of class and nobility private dances were held as well as dance events at suitable public dance venues for the well-to-do to dance their evenings or daytimes away. Hotels such as the Savoy hosted many a dance evening and daytime tea dance. London became the centre of the ball season and gained an important place in the social calendar of the elite. The Ritz greatly influenced dance-floor tastes and the popularity of dance and dance halls at the time[113] by hosting regular dance events and tea dances. Other popular clubs for the social elite in London were the Lotus Club on Garrick Street, Murray's Night Club on Soho's Beak Street and the 400 Club on Old Bond Street.[114] In the early 1950s the 400 Club is said to have been a favourite of Princess Margaret, who would sit at a regular table with friends which became known as the Royal Box.

Another popular venue was the Gargoyle Club – a private members' club at 69 Dean Street, London, which opened in 1925. It was located on the upper floors of the building

OPPOSITE Advertisement for the Palais de Danse, Hammersmith, London, from *Dancing World*, October 1920.

THOUSANDS of dancing enthusiasts visit the Palais de Danse daily.

WHY?

Simply because it is the finest dancing salon in Europe, and offers ample scope for the fullest enjoyment. It is perfectly fitted and furnished throughout, and is equipped with a resilient parquet dancing floor.

Two celebrated American Jazz Bands —acknowledged the best in the world— render the music twice daily.

80 Lady & Gentlemen instructors always in attendance.

. .

If you would know the REAL pleasures of Dancing, then you, too, must visit the Palais de Danse.

FROM DANCE HALL
TO WHITE SLAVERY

and required entrance through a lift (if you could find it), and was owned by the Scottish aristocrat David Tennant, son of the 1st Baron Glenconner. The Gargoyle was intimate and open all hours and because it was difficult to find it had an air of secrecy and exclusivity. Inside was a ballroom with a jazz orchestra, a drawing room and a rooftop terrace and bar. The artist Henri Matisse was a friend of Tennant's and is said to have been a regular visitor at the club. Matisse gifted two paintings to Tennant: *The Red Studio*, displayed in the bar, and *The Studio, Quai St Michel*, displayed on the club's stairs.[115]

From the beginning of the First World War until the late 1930s the working classes saw a shift in their financial position and working hours. Average working hours fell from fifty-four to forty-eight hours and weekly wages rose from £1 and 12 shillings in 1913 to £3 and 10 shillings in 1938. Nearly 42 per cent of workers now received holiday pay.[116] All of this gave the working class more leisure opportunities and increased the popularity of dance halls. They grew from working-class dance venues into large dance-hall chains

such as the Palais de Danse and the Palais Royale – spaces that then dominated dance tastes for the next few years. It is estimated that 11,000 dance halls and nightclubs opened throughout the UK between 1919 and 1926.[117]

Post-First World War Britain, like many countries around the world, had to face not only collective personal bereavement but also national issues such as the recovery of the economy and the rebuilding necessitated by bombing, along with fractured communities and families. Dancing helped to foster a happy, healthy nation and this in many ways became the brand of a new era of Englishness: a dancing nation and a united

OPPOSITE Front cover to *From Dance Hall to White Slavery: Stories of Actual Events, Places and Persons* by John Dillon and H. W. Lytle, 1942.

ABOVE 'Kit-Cat Club: "High Life" in the Haymarket' by Dorothea St John George, plate from *Nights in London: Where Mayfair Makes Merry* by Horace Wyndham, 1926.

"NEW PRINCES' FRIVOLITIES"

Princes' for Pleasure!

ABOVE 'New Princes' Frivolities: Princes' for Pleasure!' by Dorothea St John George, plate from *Nights in London: Where Mayfair Makes Merry* by Horace Wyndham, 1926.

BLANCHARD'S IN BEAK STREET
" Formerly Murray's "

ABOVE 'Blanchard's in Beak Street: Formerly Murray's' by Dorothea St John George, plate from *Nights in London: Where Mayfair Makes Merry* by Horace Wyndham, 1926.

South London's Magnificent New Palais.

ABOVE Photograph of 'South London's Magnificent New Palais', *Dancing Times*, November 1929.

OPPOSITE Sheet music for 'Lingering: Instrumental & Vocal Fox-Trot ... The Season's Success at the Palais de Danse, London', words by John P. Harrington, music by T. W. Thurban, c.1921.

Blighty. The dance halls gained in popularity in the lead up to the Second World War, but from 1941 clothes rationing made fashionable dressing difficult;[118] no doubt a large amount of begged, borrowed or even stolen attire was transformed into an eye-catching dance-floor outfit or two. It's hard to imagine dancing socially without giving a thought to fashion; they often come together, marking both the intention of the dancer and their social status.

Things were changing rapidly as class distinctions blurred and women gained the temporary right to ask men to dance. The issue of racial tension, however, was never far away at dance halls during the Second World War and US soldiers introduced divisive racial systems to Britain including segregation between Black and white citizens. White British dance-hall attendees could also be unwelcoming to Black soldiers, and there were outbreaks of violence.

In 1943 tensions were heightened in Central London on one particularly bad weekend. A stabbing and a shooting outside the Paramount dance hall led to a pitched battle in Leicester Square between Black and white American soldiers and between Black Americans and local whites. Paramount managers Harry Chaperlin and Carl Heimann introduced a forty-eight-hour ban on all Black people at the club 'in their own interests' for safety[119] and to calm the tension between Black and white patrons. The same Jim Crow laws that separated Black and white US soldiers during the World Wars also applied to those soldiers while they were in the UK, meaning that they could not mix socially. Dance halls had to arrange separate evenings for Black and white GIs, which was met with understandable contempt from the Black soldiers.

The dance halls survived through many dancing trends from foxtrot to rock 'n' roll, but their popularity began to decline during the transition from live bands to recorded music. The very first 45 rpm records became available in March 1949 and meant that music could be played much more conveniently in smaller venues or at home. Dancers could now more easily pick and choose their own music, so that dance halls became less attractive. The 1950s then introduced rock 'n' roll, coffee bars and a different kind of cool that would eventually mark the dismantling of dance halls as social tastes developed and changed.

OPPOSITE Photograph of an African American GI dancing with a white woman at the Bouillabaisse Club in New Compton Street, Soho, London, *Picture Post*, 17 July 1943.

A first in screening an all rock 'n' roll show on British television, *Six-Five Special* was broadcast on the BBC in 1957. It was hosted by popular disc jockey of the time Pete Murray, who would open the show with his catchphrase 'Time to jive on the old six-five' and featured artists such as Petula Clark and Tommy Steele. *Oh Boy!* (1958–9) followed on ITV and had a similar format with guest singers such as Cliff Richard and Marty Wilde. This marked a change in British dancing tastes as television became the source for youthful dances and fashions rather than the dance hall.

Ready Steady Go! (1963–6), a commercial network broadcast from ITV, showed popular bands of the day such as The Beatles along with a studio full of avid music fans and dancers who projected a cool, free-spirited approach to fashion and expressive dancing. This was in contrast to the coordinated dance steps that might be seen in dance halls[120] and marked a more relaxed attitude to dancing as well as a growing preference for nightclubs, rather than the bigger dance floors, which were seen as old-fashioned.

Today events such as festivals or raves, where thousands of people attend to hear music and dance, in some way retain the spirit of dance hall. The fashion is very different, but the common factor is a love of dance and music. There are many dance-hall buildings still in use today – mostly as music venues for live gigs or specialist events, some as discotheques, some as bingo halls – all adapting to the financial opportunities of their time.

The common experience of an awkward first partner dance as a teenager – usually at a school disco – perhaps suggests a usefulness to learning to dance in the ways of old. Understanding properness and etiquette to improve social dancing confidence might not be such a bad thing. In the nineteenth and early twentieth centuries partner dances, dance cards and court dances were designed for people to meet, to be social and to connect. As we draw closer to the mid-twenty-first century people tend to connect via social media, favouring filming their individual or group dances to be shared on screen for likes. Dancing fads will always come and go but I can't help feeling that bringing back some of the old dance-hall vibe would be a good thing.

OPPOSITE Cover to the LP 'Six-Five Special!', based on the successful BBC TV series. Parlophone (EMI) label PMC 1047, first issued 1957.

CHAPTER 09.

JIVE AND ROCK 'N' ROLL

WAR, THOUGH IT may seem unrelated to dance, has often played a role in how dance has been shaped throughout the world. The arrival of American soldiers in Britain during the Second World War symbolised the war effort as a global issue. The American GIs brought with them not only military expertise and weapons but also dance and music; their arrival demonstrated the developing nature of culture and how, through the exchange of dance, language and music, one country can have a remarkable influence on another. Jive and jitterbug were part of that cultural exchange during the Second World War.[121]

The ragtime and early jazz bandleader and composer James Reese Europe (1881-1919)[122] had brought jazz over to Britain during the First World War, adding new rhythms to the already popular syncopated ragtime and associated animal dances. In his 1939 song 'Jumpin' Jive' Cab Calloway (1907-1994) helped popularise swing music further and introduced the word 'jive' into general usage. 'Jive' was used as street slang by hipsters (also known as hepcats) and Black musicians during the time of the Harlem Renaissance to refer to someone's deceptive or foolish behaviour. Later 'turkey' was added and the term 'jive turkey' was coined, meaning someone who exaggerates, gives empty promises or is dishonest. The term was later used in song

by the Ohio Players in 'Jive Turkey' (1974) and the Bee Gees' 'Jive Talkin'' (1975).

The dance we know as jive, as we saw in Chapter 7, had morphed from jitterbug, swing and Lindy hop to become a big part of the 1930s and 1940s dancing narrative. Arriving from across the Atlantic to be received by dancers who were far removed from North America and the Black social experience from which it came, jive in Britain and many other countries was understood as simply the dance, rather than the people and history behind it.

Jive became popular in the dance halls of the 1940s and was a great accompaniment to the big-band sound of the time, created by composers and bandleaders such as Count Basie (1904-1984) and Benny Goodman (1909-1986) in the 1930s and Glenn Miller (1904-1944) in the 1940s. The shifting rhythms of swing music lit up the dance floor, framing a dance narrative that was very different from the more sedate dances and music popular at the beginnings of dance halls.

Jive is an energised partner dance with holds, leaps, lifts, turns, rocking steps, fancy footwork, a steady groove, crossing patterns and swaying hips. As it gained in popularity along with the exciting new rhythms of

OPPOSITE Photograph of dancing at Rainbow Corner, a London club for American servicemen, *Picture Post*, 27 January 1945.

the big-band sound, it quickly become mainstream and commercialised. Jive competitions were regular events in dance halls. There is a lovely clip in the Huntley Film Archives of couples dancing in a jive competition in the 1940s, filmed in black and white.[123] Unfortunately there is no sound, but the short clip captures the energy of jive in this time – the weaving of bodies and the playfulness as well as the seriousness of dancing jive in competitions, especially the male of the first dancing couple, who separates from his partner on their finish and goes into a celebratory improvised groove. The crowd is happy and jubilant, some clapping and shouting, some remaining still and retaining their cool.

Another clip, this one from the British Pathé website – 'Jive Dance 1943', filmed at the Hammersmith Palais de Danse[124] – is narrated by Josephine Bradley (see page 81), who introduces Tony Jackson and Mavis Sutton dancing a jitterbug with a lively gusto of lifts, twists, fancy steps, bent knees and hunched postures. Bradley dismisses the jitterbug as 'hardly a dance that will grace our ballrooms' before introducing Norma Cave and Jack Orton-Smith for a demonstration of jive. Cave and Orton-Smith do not demonstrate any lifts, and their steps

are much gentler and their posture straighter than that of Jackson and Sutton; this along with Bradley's running commentary in Received Pronunciation evokes the English style associated with ballroom dancing.

Bradley then asks the couples to change partners and demonstrate jive together, assuring the audience that Jackson and Sutton, now dancing jive rather than jitterbug, will be 'entirely tamed'. Audience members are asked to join them and we see a dance floor filled with people dancing jive – noticeably without any lifts. Here, just as in the nineteenth century, dance is being shaped by considerations of properness; the jitterbug is presented as being a lower dance form, while jive is a refined activity that suits ballroom tastes.

One might think that dance was less of a priority in war, but instead it triumphed and found a new home in the dance halls. Jive, jitterbug and swing became the backdrop to the Blitz. American GIs helped make sense of these new dances. Jive and jitterbug changed the dance floor and both Black and white Americans brought great inspiration to British and European dance floors from across the pond. When the Second World War ended in 1945 many US soldiers went home, but there were still US military and

OPPOSITE Sheet music for 'In the Mood', words by Andy Razaf, music by Joe Garland, performed by Glenn Miller and His Orchestra, 1939.

OPPOSITE '"There Freddy, that's what I want us to practise"', from *Swing Fever Jitterbug*, compiled by J. Mackenzie, 1942.

ABOVE 'Letting themselves go – and enjoying it!', from *Swing Fever Jitterbug*.

ABOVE 'The jitterbug "swirl" as demonstrated by Bill Mawson and Esmay Cox of Australia', from *Swing Fever Jitterbug*, compiled by J. Mackenzie, 1942.

MIDDLE 'Jim Brennan and Tessie Fekan were awarded first prize in the Ben Bernie Jitterbug Contest held in New York', from *Swing Fever Jitterbug*.

RIGHT 'Girls were flung high into the air with legs kicking into space', from *Swing Fever Jitterbug*.

air force bases in Britain. Cultural exchange continued as arriving soldiers, airmen and navy personnel brought new music such as rock 'n' roll, rhythm 'n' blues, soul and later hip hop, along with new dances to accompany them. There were of course many other ways in which rock 'n' roll spread from America, for instance radio and film, tourists, visiting musicians and American immigrants to Britain and Europe.

From waltzes to foxtrots the constant appearance of new dances had to be carefully managed. The foxtrot, first thought of as wild and dangerous, now seemed a little tame. Jive and jitterbug were more elaborate, more physical, much bolder in movement, and freer. Unlike the foxtrot, the jitterbug, jive and later rock 'n' roll brought daring lifts and much wilder, shaking bodies. At times this was seen as dangerous and air steps and lifts were banned by some venues.[125] With the dancers in full flow, the idea of going back to the steadier, calmer steps of the foxtrot would have been unthinkable. Those who sought order in the dance halls had their work cut out.

Love and the dance floor have always been entwined, and jive and jitterbug certainly had a romance about them. Maybe the war magnified an air of hope that shone through the dancers; these turning, kicking, jiving, swinging bodies of optimism saw a future of love not war. Despite this embrace of love on the dance floor, though, same-sex or gender-fluid dancing remained hidden. There is little information on this because of the social and political attitudes towards gay relationships at the time: gay sex wasn't legalised in Britain until 1967 and as a result the social aspects of gay life were very much underground.

Allan Bérubé has written about the life of American soldiers who would arrange regular private parties where they could dance and be openly gay.[126] Some of these soldiers would no doubt have come to Britain and recreated those parties or found similar ones. As the war years lingered, though homosexual acts between men remained illegal, fictional representation of gay culture in the media was slowly growing. As we will see on page 191, gay social dance eventually had its chance to be seen in the mainstream through vogue. This marked a change in the visibility of gay life and gay dancing life and a step towards equality, demonstrating the political power that dance can wield.

The new sounds of the 1950s from musicians like Bill Haley, Little Richard and Elvis Presley saw jive morph into rock 'n' roll,[127] lighting up the dance floor for an awaiting generation of teens who had yet to have their time on it. Rock 'n' roll, like its dancing ancestors, came with cool, rebellion and style. Leather jackets and James Dean

OPPOSITE 'Front cover to *Swing Fever Jitterbug*, compiled by J. Mackenzie, 1942.

swaggers were the signposts of upheaval. In Britain the teddy boys reinvented the Edwardian suit, pairing it with brothel-creeper shoes.[128] The girls, in either pencil skirts or flowing dresses, brought their own style to the dance floor.

Films such as *Blackboard Jungle* (1955) – an urban American story with a racially mixed cast and groundbreaking rock 'n' roll-infused musical soundtrack that included Bill Haley & His Comets' 'Rock Around the Clock' (1954) – would enrapture a new generation. When it was screened at a cinema in Elephant and Castle, South London in 1956 a teenage audience of teddy boys began tearing out the chairs and dancing in the aisles in response to the film. Similar responses of riotous behaviour would follow up and down the UK, leading rock 'n' roll and teddy boys to be associated with youth delinquency.

Rock 'n' roll is considered one of the twentieth century's earliest teenage subcultures. Energised by its development away from swing and the music and fashion of the 1950s, it was practised at home, at school, on the dance floor and in the dance studio by a generation who, unlike their parents, had independence and a new sense of hope. They did not want to dress as their monochrome parents did. They wanted colour, light, music, dancing and sexual liberation. Just like Lindy hop before it, rock 'n' roll was a spectacle dance. The groove, the lifts, the attitude were cultivated and required practice, though of course one could casually two-step or bop on the side without the fancy moves.

Rock 'n' roll dancing was not always about energised fancy steps, turns and lifts. It also accompanied love songs at a slower tempo such as The Penguins' 'Earth Angel (Will You Be Mine)' (1954) or The Flamingos' 'I Only Have Eyes For You' (1959). The dynamic steps were set aside to match the mood and the music of romance, somewhat reminiscent of the foxtrot from decades earlier, but slower and with an edge. Rock 'n' roll dancing also included the hand jive, which involved movements such as circling

ABOVE Poster for the film *Blackboard Jungle*, 1955.

OPPOSITE 'The Truth about the "Teddy Boys" and the Teddy Girls', *Picture Post*, 29 May 1954. The photograph shows a couple at the Tottenham Mecca dance hall in North London.

THE TRUTH ABOUT

THE 'TEDDY BOYS'

AND THE TEDDY GIRLS

The 'Edwardians,' or 'Teddy Boys,' have been branded as hooligans, juvenile gangsters and delinquents. They have also been called dandies and mother's darlings. It is a confusing picture of exaggeration and distortion. A PICTURE POST *investigation seeks to bring it into focus. Our staff writer,* HILDE MARCHANT, *presents the facts. A* PSYCHIATRIST *of much experience with young people, interprets them.* JOSEPH McKEOWN *took the pictures*

THE SUIT THAT GRANDFATHER MIGHT HAVE WORN
The dance is contemporary jive. But the suit is an adaptation of the Edwardian 'masher's' outfit. It is also English in conception and, unlike recent men's fashions, owes nothing to Hollywood.

WE were in a dance-hall in Tottenham—a suburb of London—and the young men we wished to contact were distinctive and obvious. The floppy jackets hung to their knees, the poplin shirts were advertisement white, the trousers were ankle tight, the shoes were good black leather, and the ties were narrow bows. An ugly outfit? That is a matter of opinion; and we were not seeking opinion—only facts. To approach the facts meant we had first to approach the boys, talk to them, and challenge the honesty of their talk. And the first thing that struck me was that their clothes are deceptive. This Edwardian fashion gives a uniformity to a group of young people who are far from uniform. They are as varied, diverse and informal as any other group of human beings. They set a pattern in their velvet collars, dog-tooth checks and moccasin shoes. But there is no such standard pattern about their lives or behaviour.

But let them talk for themselves, for they are frank enough. What do they do during the day, or the week? One is a toy maker, one a glass cutter. Another is an engineer's apprentice, one a die cutter, another an electric welder and surprisingly, another a National Serviceman on leave—back in his Teddy Boy civilian 'uniform.' (His hair was shorter than the others, but would still have horrified the Sergeant-major.) Their wages were good—ranging from the £4 17s. 6d. a week apprentice, to just over £12 a week for the skilled cabinet maker. Their suits cost between £17 and £20. All of them agreed that a good poplin shirt was just under £2 and that a pair of shoes was around the £3 mark. Most of them 'kept themselves'; which means they pay their parents something towards the rent and the household budget. Even so, pocket money was never less than £2 a week, and often double. They were not interested in drink—a beer, perhaps, but more likely a mineral water. They

an index finger, hitching-a-ride gestures and fist pounding, and was often danced to set choreography.[129] Hand jive even had its own song with Johnny Otis's 'Willie and the Hand Jive' (1958), and a choreographed hand jive was later performed in the film *Grease* (1978). This style shows a teenage goofiness in stark contrast to the image of violent or otherwise delinquent rock 'n' roll.

Another dance associated with rock 'n' roll is the Madison, which appeared on dance floors in the late 1950s. It consists of a series of choreographed group dances that always start with the left leg forward, developing into a back-and-forth stepping and clapping motion accompanied by gestures such as the clicking of fingers. It has roots in African American communities and, while some accounts give its place of invention as Detroit, Michigan or Indiana, the most cited source is the LVA Club, a Black social club in Columbus, Ohio. William 'Bubbles' Holloway, who coached young dancers at the club, had just returned from a trip to New York, where he had asked for directions to Madison Avenue and been told to 'take it to the left'. He reportedly recalled the term when teaching and used stepping with the left foot forward as the basis for creating the Madison.

The Madison was danced in a forward-facing formation similar to line dancing, which recalled its lineage of country dances, or contra dances, a century or more earlier.[130] It was made famous in 1960 on the *Buddy Deane Show* in the US[131] and through various recordings that promoted the dance. The Madison later featured in the Hollywood film *Hairspray* (1988), which explores teenage self-expression in the 1960s to a backdrop of a racialised America in which Black dances are appropriated on mainstream television for a white audience.

As music changed and the 1960s dawned, the arrival of The Beatles and the English invasion of the United States were to add another challenge to the dance floor. The commercialisation of rock 'n' roll saw teen-orientated rhythms and poster-perfect pop stars rule the airwaves. Rock 'n' roll then merged into rock music with a harder face that was far removed from teen pop bands: a head-banging feast of long hair and unkempt clothes with anti-pop revolution as its goal.

OPPOSITE Poster for the film *Rock Around the Clock*, 1956.

ABOVE Photograph of dancing in the street after a screening of *Rock Around the Clock*, *The Sphere*, 22 September 1956.

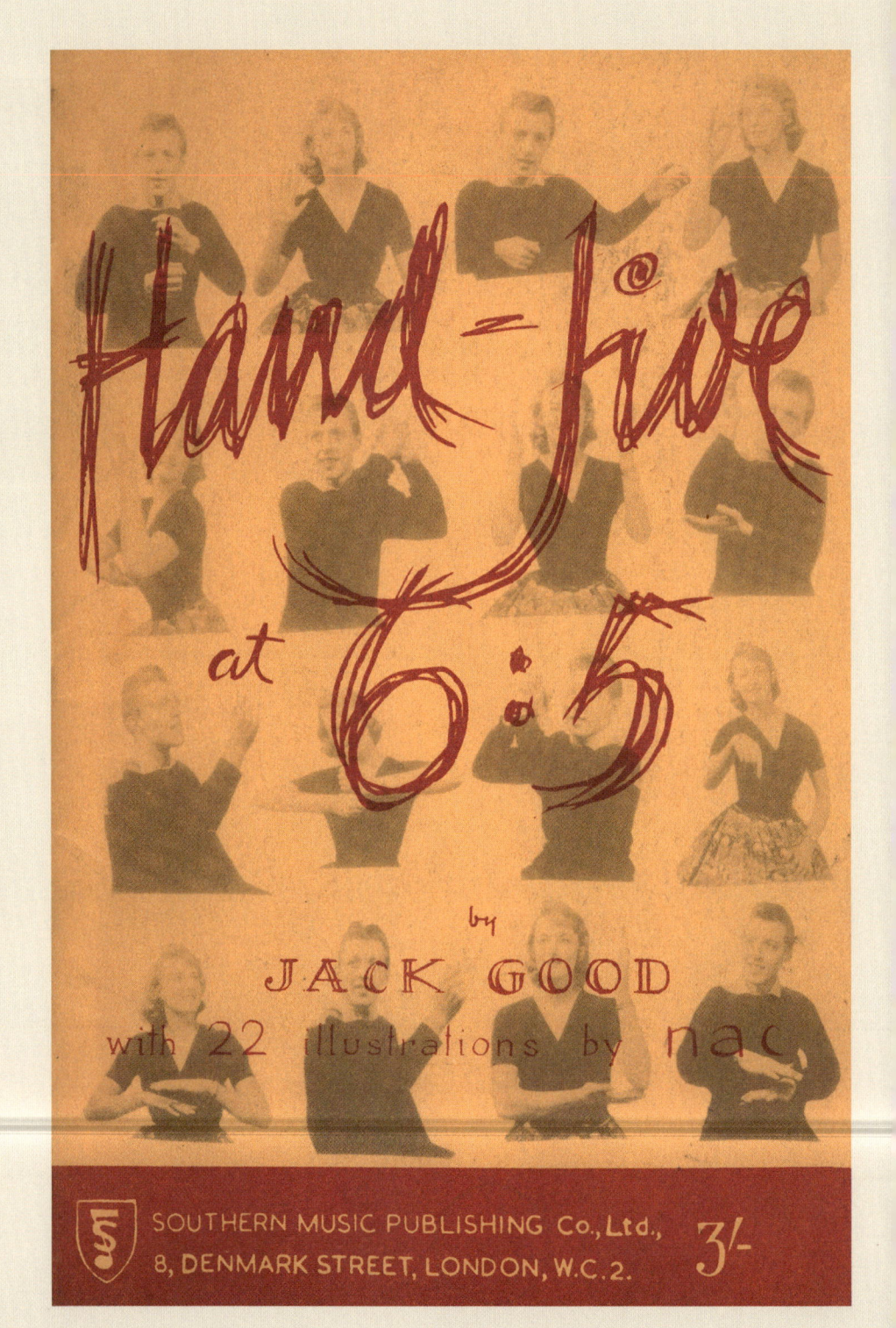

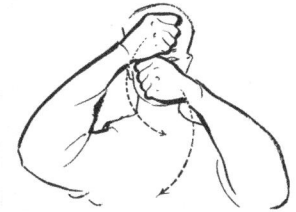

"The Steps"
Fists clenched as for the climb. The right fist is held up level with the forehead. Then the left fist is placed under it, little finger of the right hand touching forefinger of the left hand. Now the right fist is withdrawn and placed under the left fist, which in turn is placed under the right fist. Finally the right fist again goes under the left, so the fists are by now at chest level. (Two bars.)

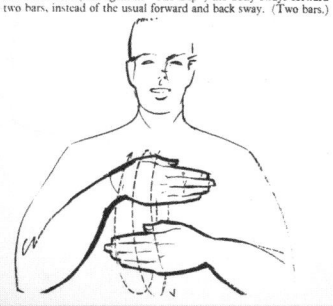

"Over the Points"
The hands are outstretched with the palms facing the chest, knuckles outwards and with the right hand in front of the left. Now the hands circle round each other as the arms are slowly outstretched. In this movement (and again in "The Dip") the body sways forward for two bars, instead of the usual forward and back sway. (Two bars.)

Some rock 'n' roll dancers grew tired of the over-saturation that was to mark its demise, turning to new inspirations such as mod, now favouring the sounds of modernist jazz rather than rock 'n' roll. Mod is probably known less for its invention of dance and more for its peacock posturing alongside the drugs and all-nighters; its spirit is most notably captured in the film *Quadrophenia* (1979). Mod, or at least some mods, then grew tired of its popular appeal and sought new inspiration, turning to then rare soul music and what would develop into northern soul.

Northern soul was a Black music based subculture that came out of northern England in the late 1960s. Dave Godin, who ran a record shop in Covent Garden, London, noticed visiting soul enthusiasts from northern England asking for rare soul records with a similar feel and tempo and began to refer to these particular records as northern soul – inadvertently giving northern soul its name. Records that fitted the northern soul framework were a mix of soulful vocals and syncopated beats – songs like Gloria Jones's 'Tainted Love' (1964).

Northern soul at its heart offered working-class people of the north of England a space to dance away from the gloom of the early 1970s. All-night dancing, rhythmic footwork, shuffles, extreme spins, jumps and leaps ruled the northern dance floors[132] – spins and leaps that held traces of Lindy hop preserved in rock 'n' roll such as improvisational moments within a breakaway as the dancers split from their partners and peacocked their best moves.

Lindy hop's legacy continued through swing, jive and jitterbug, rock 'n' roll and even, though less overtly, northern soul. Like mod, northern soul was exclusive, a place for the in-crowd and a precursor to modern clubbing. In the 1960s and 1970s, just as with jive and jitterbug in earlier decades, a new generation were finding their independence through a dancing revolution.

OPPOSITE Front cover to *Hand-Jive at 6:5* by Jack Good, 1958.

ABOVE Diagrams of the moves of the hand jive, 'The Steps' and 'Over the Points', from *Hand-Jive at 6:5*.

CHAPTER 10.

DANCE CRAZES AND DANCE-FLOOR COOL

WHEN DANCE IS exposed to the limelight it can burn out very quickly. The centuries of lost dances teach us that a dance being considered a fad or craze usually leads to a single doorway labelled 'exit'. Dances such as the Mashed Potato, Time Warp, Macarena and Gangnam Style were created for quick record sales. Some are temporarily revived for pop videos to evoke a sense of nostalgia that introduces the featured singers to new audiences. The video released in 2021 for Harry Styles's song 'Treat People with Kindness' takes its audience back to an eclectic mix of 1970s Davie Bowie-style glam rock and Fred Astaire and Ginger Rogers-inspired nostalgia. In the same year Little Mix's 'Confetti' combined tropes from 1990s rap videos with a performance of camp reminiscent of Tina Turner.

Discotheques and nightclubs excited dance floors throughout the 1970s; they commanded prime-time slots on TV, featured in blockbuster films and gave rock music a run for its money on the radio. The hustle, a Latin partner dance, came to symbolise disco; it is believed to have originated in New York around 1970 in mostly Puerto Rican neighbourhoods. The hustle contained elements of other Latin dances carried to the United States such as cha cha cha and mambo, and it epitomised the commercial disco era along with under-developed two-steps and medallion-chested men. New York clubs like the Loft or Sanctuary were forgotten;[133] forward-thinking clubs with a mix of sexualities and genders – an inclusive experience – dominated disco and club life as early as 1970. These underground innovators were later cast aside or chose to remain outcasts as disco went mainstream.

John Travolta and *Saturday Night Fever* (1977) were seen by many as the catalysts for disco around the world. In reality the film was a feat of misdirection in both the history of disco and the stories of the Loft and Sanctuary. John Travolta's famous arm points, projecting his disco cool and working-class hero status, hid the true history of those famous arm moves. He was really trying to lock.

Locking, originally Campbell locking, was a dance developed by Don 'Campbellock' Campbell (1951–2020) in the early 1970s in Los Angeles, California – a funky dance with sharp poses, points, hat tricks and a give-yourself-five handclap. Don Campbell initially showcased his talent on the

OPPOSITE Photograph of people on the dance floor at a club, c.1975.

television programme *Soul Train* as a solo dancer and went on to form The Lockers, an all-Black male dance group apart from Toni Basil, who was white and female. Not known in Britain at the time, The Lockers danced on many prime-time shows in the United States throughout the 1970s. The original group broke up in 1977, but Toni Basil later released the song *Hey Mickey* (1981) and Don Campbell continued the group with new members.

Adolfo 'Shabba Doo' Quinones (1955–2020) from The Lockers appeared in the film *Breakdance* (1984; released under the title *Breakin'* in the United States). Fred Berry had success in the United States in the TV show *What's Happening!!* (1976–9). Before the film *Breakdance* and the explosion of hip hop in the early 1980s little was known about The Lockers and locking outside the United States, other than in Japan as some of the early locking pioneers toured there in the 1970s.

What does this have to do with John Travolta and *Saturday Night Fever*? Part of Travolta's famous dance scene in the film was taught to him by Deney Terrio, a second-generation locker, who had learnt locking from Don Campbell. Travolta's tuition included knee drops with folded arms and Russian-type kicks in a low squat position, kicking out one leg in time to the music, which Terrio got from The Lockers. One move in particular, known as Uncle Sam Points, which mimics the poster of the same name, was inscribed into the zeitgeist of the time, but not as a locking move. Travolta reframed the Uncle Sam Points in his solo as his own signature move – pointing towards the floor and ceiling then scanning the room with a brooding gaze. Had John Travolta demonstrated Uncle Sam Points the Don Campbell way, popular dance history would have been very different.[134]

This is just one of many times that dance has been appropriated without acknowledgement when it has moved into the realm of the commercial. The roots of Travolta's dance moves in the film are not something most people would take time to find out about; such a detail usually only concerns dancers, teachers, researchers and cultural enthusiasts. It is a familiar story of the Black contribution to popular culture, much like that of Lindy hop, one in which history favours fame and commercial success over the anonymous true creative artists whose dance moves are cultivated out of sight at nightclubs or parties.

In 1970s Britain punk and northern soul were all the rage along with David Bowie and glam rock. Simmering away in the

OPPOSITE Karen Lynn Gorney and John Travolta on the poster for the film *Saturday Night Fever*, 1977.

FOLLOWING PAGES Photograph of The Lockers by Jean-Paul Goude, from *Esquire* magazine.

background was jazz funk.[135] This was an expressive party dance from Black British club dancers that mixed disco steps, groovy two-steps, curved bending torsos and captivating poses. The British funk group Hi-Tension in their 1978 song of the same name encapsulated the jazz-funk scene of 1970s and early 1980s Britain.

Jazz-funk dance shifted in musical taste and tempo from the funk sounds of Earth, Wind & Fire towards jazz fusion, hard bop and Latin jazz in tracks such as Art Blakey's 'A Night in Tunisia' (1960). Fast-paced footwork like soft-shoe tap and multiple knee spins marked British jazz dancers' identity as separate from African American footwork, which was similar but did not have the Black British flavour underneath it – a mix of jazz funk and reggae skanking steps and posture. Dance groups like IDJ[136] and Brothers in Jazz[137] dominated UK jazz dance through the 1980s.

Sadly UK jazz dance from this era is slowly disappearing from British dance floors, hit hard by changing dance-floor tastes such as house music as well as isolating itself through its own elitist dance-floor culture. UK jazz dance, like many other dance-floor trends, has fallen out of favour. Japanese dance enthusiasts picked up the mantle in the late 1980s and early 1990s, though, and in Japan

the UK style of jazz dance is a regular sight in clubs and on stage.

Both IDJ and Brothers in Jazz performed in Japan in the late 1980s and left their mark on Japanese street-dance culture. In 1990 a dance group from Japan called Sound Cream Steppers won a competition to train with Brothers in Jazz in London.[138] The migration of UK jazz dance to Japan was potentially its saviour; the Japanese street-dance community is taking on the role of cultural conduit by evolving UK jazz dance as their own style and developing a new community and home for it.

It's not just hip hop or street dance that get people on the floor today. Square dances and line dances, enjoyed from community centres to ballrooms, still take place regularly with the most enthusiastic participants. Both square and line dances have roots, like many of the other dances in this book, in European formation dances such as the cotillion and country dance.[139] These American dances mirror the carefully structured spatial patterns and unified lines of *contredanses* through pre-set group formations and structured steps that reveal the deep origins of line and square dancing.

Line dancing, associated mostly with country music, cowboy boots and Stetsons, is one

OPPOSITE Photograph of 'Brothers in Jazz' at the Royal College of Art by Peter Williams, 1988.

of those social dances that time permits brief spells of popularity. There is a great joy to be had in social group dancing. Just as with the quadrilles and cotillions of older times it takes a lot of commitment for the enthusiast to learn the extensive range of vocabulary, steps and set choreography that form square and line dancing, but there is a considerable pay-off. The group momentum in line dancing is a thrill and a big part of its attraction – multiple bodies in symmetrical lines stepping forward, back, turning left in unison in some ways similar to double-work or *pas de deux*, in which you turn around and catch your partner in the air. It's as if the universe is focused on you and your dance partner.

Mosh pits, punk, air guitar, head banging, skanking, dancehall, krump, house, rave,

phone waving and even dad dancing are all part of the dancing world. They are carefully coded moments of movement that demonstrate a collective understanding of place, music and motion. Abstract, cool, unorthodox, weird and beautiful, social dancing offers an insight into the many facets of human behaviour and shows the variety of the human form. When dancing is seen without music it often looks unorthodox or weird; the magical thing is when the music is on there is a beautiful transformation as the movements of the dancer instantly make sense.

The electric slide, also known as the Candy dance, is still danced at many a party around the world when the 1986 song 'Candy' by Cameo is played. I can only describe the electric slide as a soul dance version of line dancing. The first few bars signal a soon-to-be-filled dance floor and a collective choreography of joy, happiness and togetherness fills the space. What the electric slide demonstrates is how the collective memory of a community can be danced and passed down generations as cultural knowledge and tradition with little regard for what is popular or mainstream. The electric slide isn't about the individual or showing off; it's about sharing tradition in communities and across generations.

ABOVE Cover to the LP 'Music for Jazz Dancers', Freestyle Records, 2010.

In 1980s Britain a mirror image of the tango was played out on the dance floor in lovers rock, a British genre of music and dance inspired by reggae. Slow and smooth rhythms in songs like Janet Kay's 'Silly Games' (1979) instigated a partner dance of hip to hip, leg to leg, cheek to cheek and groin to groin. This dance requires as little space as possible between the two dancing bodies – a winding, grinding motion of intimacy that many thought belonged in the bedroom. Like tango, lovers rock demonstrates sexual motivation as an integral part of dance culture.

Unlike the dance halls and ballrooms of the early nineteenth century, where dancing masters ensured properness, nightclubs, discos and raves are mostly unpoliced when it comes to how you dance. Sexuality on the dance floor has always been present, whether covert or overt. From molly houses – gay social spaces of the nineteenth century[140] – to dance venues in London's Soho frequented by the artist Francis Bacon (1909–1992) in the 1960s,[141] dance is an invitation to all.

Vogue, a dance originating in New York's gay culture, mirrors the poses and posturing of old film stars on the cover of *Vogue* magazine with complex symmetrical and asymmetrical lines and gestures and is the best-known style

in overground gay dance culture.[142] Another style is waacking, a dance created by Black and Latino gay dancers in the early 1970s in Los Angeles, California. While vogue is based on the image and poses, waacking is based on a dramatic and visceral expression of emotion through dance, a form of storytelling. Vogue can be more staccato in its movements with more complex patterns, whereas waacking flows in and out of flurries of arm movements and wrist rolls into sharp intense poses and outward emotion.

Madonna's 1990 song 'Vogue' and the accompanying video with the vogue style exploded into the mainstream. The roots of vogue precede Madonna and can be traced back to the Harlem Renaissance. Black gay men who escaped the poverty and racism of the South found their way to the excitement of Harlem. Balls offered the chance for open queerness and became places of escape in which these men could express themselves freely. The Savoy Ballroom hosted such events.[143] It is also thought that vogue balls have roots in prison culture and took place at Rikers Island, New York's jail at this time; gay inmates would reportedly hold vogue balls that aimed to mirror the balls held in the Savoy Ballroom.

The documentary *Paris Is Burning* (1990) is a very insightful record not only of vogue, but

also of New York of that time and features Willi Ninja of House of Ninja. Part of vogue's framework is the house system, inspired by the fashion houses of haute couture, with House of Ninja being one of the most prominent. Another documentary, *Strike a Pose* (2016), continues vogue's story, giving an account of the dancers in Madonna's 'Vogue' video, one of temporary media success that faded as Madonna moved on to her next image. As its home shifted from disco and vogue balls[144] to music videos screened on MTV, vogue shone brightly in popular view for a while. But eventually its light burnt out; it was seen as a dance craze and it disappeared from the mainstream.

However temporary its time in the mainstream vogue marked a change in the visibility of gay life and specifically gay dancing life. Unlike the 2012 South Korean novelty dance Gangnam Style vogue is more than a three-minute fad; it's a whole universe of social and cultural systems. The difficulty for vogue, like many underground dance forms, is that its dancers were naively unprepared for the world lens; the currency of vogue was exported from familiar underground spaces onto the world stage, where for a moment it seemed like its creators were winning, only for it to fall

out of favour a short while later. Hip hop and breaking faced similar journeys: further underground dance movements given light, then shade, then dark.

In the mid- to late 1980s the first wave of hip hop including locking, popping and breaking also lost its popularity – a dismissal without warning into darkness for those dancers who once wowed the world with spectacular spins, but were now devalued and having to adjust to life without their dance culture. Breaking in the 1970s and 1980s captured fragments of past dances whether knowingly or not. Some steps developed after being exposed to new music and different rhythms, galvanised by the competitive nature of breaking which required a quick turnover of surprising moves.

Cholly Atkins (1913–2003), a hoofer – tap dancer and vaudeville performer – who became the house choreographer for the Motown Record label, took tap, jazz and social steps and remodelled them for Motown groups such as the Temptations and the Supremes to achieve the slick performance required by Berry Gordy for his label. By modifying tap and social dance steps, Atkins made clear how

OPPOSITE Photograph of vogue dancers Derrick Xtravaganza Huggins (bottom) and Cesar Valentino performing at the Copacabana nightclub, New York, 25 May 1989.

African American social dances of the past can re-emerge in different eras in subtle ways, such as in hip hop and breaking.[145]

Certain movements in breaking and top rock developed through dancers mimicking martial-art gestures in kung fu films. Some were passed from generation to generation through social dancing, where steps were learnt in the moment without a written manual or history, motivated by music, competition or accident. As with Josephine Baker in the 1930s, the dancers' character and style were at the forefront of their dancing.

Rock Steady Crew,[146] the famed breaking crew from the Bronx and Harlem, exploded onto the screen with a hypnotising visual impact that rocked the world. They can be seen in the video for Malcolm McLaren's song 'Buffalo Gals' (1982) and in the Hollywood film *Flashdance* (1983) – a short feature of just under one minute and thirty seconds that would change the dancing world. The song '(Hey You) The Rock Steady Crew' (1983) gifted them momentary commercial fame and a world tour. Their battle with another famed breaking crew, the New York City Breakers, in the film *Beat Street* (1984) set many a youth around the world on a summer mission of grazes, bumps, bruises and head spins. *Beat Street* was a commercial response to breaking. (The term 'breakdance', a media misquote of the time, has been mostly erased by the breaking community because it doesn't relate to its cultural history.)

Breaking was everywhere before it too lost popularity in what is known as the winter period of breaking. Rock Steady, like many other active breaking groups and enthusiasts, were put to rest. But in the early to mid-1990s breaking reframed itself and experienced a resurgence of interest. VHS tapes were the order of the day – treasured footage passed from country to country helped tie the fractured community of breaking back together and it reshaped itself with a more determined confidence. Breaking, now helped by the internet, was able to mediate itself and control its own values and vision for its future. Today breaking is regularly seen around the world, with millions of views on social media and TV shows. Dance competitions with big sponsorship deals mean breaking is big business. It is an official sport in the 2024 Olympic Games in Paris, a great milestone that will test public perceptions of breaking as a culture or sport. At the same time, it

OPPOSITE Photograph of members of the Rock Steady Crew breaking in the yard of Booker T. Washington Junior High School (JHS 54), New York, 8 May 1983.

constitutes a source of conflict between those within the hip hop community who prefer breaking in its traditional form, performed in accessible social spaces, and those who support its Olympic journey.

Rock Steady Crew were a commercial phenomenon in the 1980s, as were other dance groups such as The Lockers (see page 185). The Electric Boogaloos from Fresno and Long Beach, California, were innovators of popping who influenced Michael Jackson and taught him some of his dance moves. The MOPTOPS, now known as Elite Force, set the trail for hip hop social dance as choreography in pop videos with artists such as Mariah Carey, Will Smith and Michael Jackson. These dance innovators laid the foundations for street dance as the industry we know today, triggering new opportunities for street dance in the mainstream and paving the way for street-dance groups like Diversity, who won *Britain's Got Talent* in 2009 and became household names.

There are some dance steps, movements and gestures that float in and out of fashion. From waltzes to foxtrots, they merge with other styles and reappear in the most subtle ways. The remixing and morphing of dance is a continuous transmission of histories, and dancers carry these histories, passing style, identity and political power across national borders and down the generations. Breaking encapsulates this transmission, proving that it's much more than just spinning on your head – albeit with style.

Street and hip hop dance came from dancers within the African diaspora mixing fragments of African memory preserved in rhythms and movements with European melodies. Breaking holds stories written in invisible ink that become visible only through dancing and this is the case for dances familiar all over the world. By learning about their roots and hidden stories we can appreciate the richness and resilience of dancing culture. History tells us the commercialisation of dance can be both its worst enemy and its best friend. But I see and have experienced unity and difference coexisting through dance regardless of its commercial success. Street dance has lived many lives and, like all the other dances in the book, I wish it a better, brighter and more sustainable future. Peace.

OPPOSITE Photograph of members of the Rock Steady Crew breaking in the yard of Booker T. Washington Junior High School (JHS 54), New York, 8 May 1983. The group's co-founder Richard 'Crazy Legs' Colon (red sleeves, rear right) performs with others.

CHAPTER 11.

LAST THOUGHTS

WITH THE BLACK MIRROR at our fingertips the next dance craze is digitally never far away. It's a wonderful thing, although if media-based dance were to be the only way to watch dance, it would make me a little sad. Parties, dance studios, festivals, theatre – the dark unknown doorways where the soon-to-be-seen simmer – are what excites me. There's nothing quite like real-life dancing: people meeting, exchanging and evolving, where rivalry may turn into friendships and discovery of rhythm redefines movement through new thought and ideas. These are the places I like, where I came from and in fact where all the dances in this book came into being, through human interaction, creativity, connection and self-expression.

During the Covid-19 pandemic dancing socially was, for the most part, banned. Places of dance became increasingly fragile economically; some have not survived. I'm not just talking about nightclubs; there are also theatre and community spaces where dance of different kinds exists. Some of the more traditional or folk dances that happen in small spaces may not last or have been put on pause while they find a new home.

I hope when you read this book that you were as inspired and informed as I was researching and writing it. What's exciting about dance is that in twenty years, ten years or even five – new dances will have evolved,

making their mark and redefining how we as humans can express ourselves through dance. More than anything I look forward to great dancing in the future.

Dance will no doubt always sit beside commerce and politics as the longest-running duet of all time. It pits conflict against happiness – the tango of life. Moments of dance innovation often coincide with those of race, gender, class and sexual liberation struggles and the history of dance is inevitably bound up with slavery and many other atrocities of human behaviour. But as the study of dance expands in the twenty-first century it is helped along by mass connectivity through the internet. The opportunity to study non-European history is growing. The murder of George Floyd in 2020 and the re-emergence of the Black Lives Matter movement led to a wider visibility of Black history; the dominance of whiteness in education is being challenged as new generations seek equality by understanding the past as a way to develop new lived possibilities, in the dance world and beyond.

There is much to reflect on and much to enjoy in the history of dance. It teaches us about the experience of being human and why we should appreciate not just the dance but the people. Dance is a breath I think we all need, a breath that can invigorate the spirit and remind us change is possible. Here's to the future.

Dance with love, dance with style,

Robert

SELECT BIBLIOGRAPHY

Andrews, George Reid, *Afro-Latin America, 1800-2000*, Oxford: Oxford University Press, 2004.

Badger, Reid, *A Life in Ragtime: A Biography of James Reese Europe*, Oxford: Oxford University Press, 1995.

Bailey, Marlon M., *Butch Queens Up in Pumps: Gender, Performance, and Ballroom Culture in Detroit*, Ann Arbor: University of Michigan Press, 2016.

Baim, Jo, *Tango: Creation of a Cultural Icon*, Bloomington: Indiana University Press, 2007.

Baker, Jean-Claude and Chase, Chris, *Josephine: The Hungry Heart*, Lanham: Cooper Square Press, 2001.

Bérubé, Allan, *Coming Out Under Fire: The History of Gay Men and Women in World War II*, Chapel Hill: University of North Carolina Press, 2010.

Brooks, Lynn Matluck, *Women's Work: Making Dance in Europe Before 1800*, Madison: University of Wisconsin Press, 2007.

Browning, Barbara, *Samba: Resistance in Motion*, Bloomington: Indiana University Press, 1995.

Calabria, Frank M., *Dance of the Sleepwalkers: The Dance Marathon Fad*, Madison: University of Wisconsin Press, 1993.

Caravantes, Peggy, *The Many Faces of Josephine Baker: Dancer, Singer, Activist, Spy*, Chicago: Chicago Review Press, 2015.

Chang, Jeff, *Can't Stop Won't Stop*, New York: St Martin's Press, 2005.

Coffield, Darren, *Tales from the Colony Room: Soho's Last Bohemia*, London: Unbound, 2020.

Cole, Daniel James and Deihl, Nancy, *The History of Modern Fashion From 1850*, London: Laurence King Publishing, 2015.

Constantine, Elaine and Sweeney, Gareth, *Northern Soul: An Illustrated History*, London: Virgin Books, 2013.

Cotgrove, Mark 'Snowboy', *From Jazz Funk & Fusion to Acid Jazz: The History of the UK Jazz Dance Scene*, London: Chaser Publications, 2009.

Damon, S. Foster, *The History of Square-Dancing*, Barre Massachusetts, 1957.

Dancetime Publications, https://dancetimepublications.com/, accessed 16 February 2021.

Daniel, Yvonne, *Rumba: Dance and Social Change in Contemporary Cuba Blacks in the Diaspora*, Bloomington: Indiana University Press, 1995.

Davis, Kathy, *Dancing Tango: Passionate Encounters in a Globalizing World*, New York: New York University Press, 2015.

Dickens, Charles, *American Notes for General Circulation: Volume 1*, Cambridge: Cambridge University Press, 2009 (originally printed in 1842).

Emery, Lynne Fauley, *Black Dance: From 1619 to Today*, Princeton: Princeton Book Company, 1988.

Engelhardt, Molly, *Dancing Out of Line: Ballrooms, Ballets, and Mobility in Victorian Fiction and Culture*, Athens: Ohio University Press, 2009.

Flores, Juan, *From Bomba to Hip-Hop: Puerto Rican Culture and Latino Identity*, New York: Columbia University Press, 2000.

Foley, Catherine E., *Step Dancing in Ireland: Culture and History*, Farnham: Ashgate Publishing, 2013.

Foster, Susan Leigh, *Choreographing Empathy: Kinesthesia in Performance*, London and New York: Routledge, 2011.

Gaunt, Kyra, *The Games Black Girls Play*, New York: New York University Press, 2006.

George, Nelson, *Soul Train: The Music, Dance, and Style of a Generation*, New York: William Morrow, 2014.

Giordano, Ralph G., *Country & Western Dance (The American Dance Floor)*, Santa Barbara: Greenwood, 2011.

Glass, Barbara S., *African American Dance: An Illustrated History*, Jefferson: McFarland & Company, 2007.

Golden, Eve, *Vernon and Irene Castle's Ragtime Revolution*, Lexington: University Press of Kentucky, 2007.

Gonzalez, Mike and Yanes, Marianella, *Tango: Sex and Rhythm of the City*, London: Reaktion Books, 2013.

Gottschild, Brenda Dixon, *Waltzing in the Dark: African American Vaudeville and Race Politics in the Swing Era*, New York: St Martin's Press, 2000.

Gottschild, Brenda Dixon, *The Black Dancing Body: A Geography From Coon to Cool*, London: Palgrave Macmillan, 2003.

Gough, Melinda J., *Dancing Queen: Marie de Médicis' Ballets at the Court of Henri IV*, Toronto: University of Toronto Press, 2019.

Hancock, Black Hawk, *American Allegory: Lindy Hop and the Racial Imagination*, Chicago: University of Chicago Press, 2013.

Harman, Vicki, *The Sexual Politics of Ballroom Dancing*, London: Palgrave Macmillan, 2019.

Hazzard-Gordon, Katrina, *Jookin': The Rise of Social Dance Formations in African-American Culture*, Philadelphia: Temple University Press, 1990.

Hennessy, Kathryn and Fischel, Anna, eds., *Fashion: The Definitive History of Costume and Style*, London: Dorling Kindersley, 2013.

Henry, Dollie and Jenkins, Paul, *The Essential Guide To Jazz Dance*, Marlborough: Crowood Press, 2019.

Hodkinson, Paul and Deicke, Wolfgang, *Youth Cultures: Scenes, Subcultures and Tribes*, London: Routledge, 2007.

Howard, Skiles, *The Politics of Courtly Dancing in Early Modern England*, Amherst: University of Massachusetts Press, 1998.

Johnson, Stephen, *Burnt Cork Traditions and Legacies of Blackface Minstrelsy*, Amherst: University of Massachusetts Press 2012.

Jones, Leroi, *Blues People: Negro Music in White America*, New York: Harper Perennial, 2002.

Kant, Marion, ed., *The Cambridge Companion to Ballet*, Cambridge: Cambridge University Press, 2007.

King-Dorset, Rodreguez, *Black Dance in London, 1730–1850: Innovation, Tradition and Resistance*, Jefferson: McFarland & Company, 2008.

Laban, Rudolf, *Choreutics*, Binsted: Dance Books, 2011.

LaMothe, Kimerer L., *Why We Dance: A Philosophy of Bodily Becoming*, New York: Columbia University Press, 2015.

Lawrence, Tim, *Love Saves the Day: A History of American Dance Music Culture, 1970-1979*, Durham: Duke University Press, 2003.

Lott, Eric, *Love & Theft: Blackface Minstrelsy and The American Working Class*, Oxford: Oxford University Press, 2013.

McCoy, Horace, *They Shoot Horses, Don't They?*, London: Serpent's Tail, 2010 (originally written in 1935).

McEvenue, Kelley, *The Alexander Technique for Actors*, London: Methuen Publishing, 2001.

Martin, Carol J., *Dance Marathons: Performing American Culture of the 1920s and 1930s*, Jackson: University Press of Mississippi, 1994.

Miller, Norma and Jensen, Evette, *Swingin' at the Savoy: The Memoir of a Jazz Dancer*, Philadelphia: Temple University Press, 1996.

Mounsey, Chris and Gonda, Caroline, *Queer People: Negotiations and Expressions of Homosexuality, 1700-1800*, Lewisburg: Bucknell University Press, 2007.

Neal, Mark Anthony and Forman, Murray, *That's the Joint! The Hip-Hop Studies Reader*, London: Routledge, 2004.

Norton, Rictor, *Mother Clap's Molly House: The Gay Subculture in England, 1700-1830*, London: Gay Men's Press, 1992.

Nott, James, *Going to the Palais: A Social and Cultural History of Dancing and Dance Halls in Britain, 1918-1960*, Oxford: Oxford University Press, 2015.

Nowell, David, *The Story of Northern Soul: A Definitive History of the Dance Scene That Refuses to Die*, London: Portico, 2011.

Osumare, Halifu, *The Africanist Aesthetic in Global Hip-Hop Power Moves*, London: Palgrave Macmillan, 2007.

Owens, Thomas, *Bebop: The Music and Its Players*, Oxford: Oxford University Press, 1995.

Peppiatt, Michael, *Francis Bacon in Your Blood: A Memoir*, London: Bloomsbury Publishing, 2015.

Picart, Caroline Joan S., *From Ballroom to DanceSport: Aesthetics, Athletics, and Body Culture*, Albany: State University of New York Press, 2006.

Playford, John, *The English Dancing Master: or, plaine and easie rules for the dancing of country dances, with the tune to each dance*, Binsted: Dance Books, 2013 (originally published 1623–86?).

Powell, Anastasia, *Sex, Power and Consent: Youth Culture and the Unwritten Rules*, Cambridge: Cambridge University Press, 2010.

Price, Emmett George, *Hip Hop Culture*, Santa Barbara: ABC-CLIO, 2006.

Riis, Thomas L., *Just Before Jazz: Black Musical Theater in New York, 1890 to 1915*, Washington D.C.: Smithsonian Institution Press, 1989.

Robinson, Danielle, *Modern Moves: Dancing Race During the Ragtime and Jazz Eras*, New York: Oxford University Press, 2015.

Rose, Tricia, *The Hip Hop Wars*, New York: Basic Books, 2008.

Savage, Jon, *Teenage: The Prehistory of Youth Culture 1875-1945*, London: Penguin Books, 2008, pp. 315-34.

Savigliano, Marta E., *Tango and the Political Economy of Passion*, Boulder: Westview Press, 1995.

Saxon, Theresa, *In Dahomey in England: A (Negative) Transatlantic Performance Heritage*, University of Central Lancaster, 2015. Available at: http://clok. uclan.ac.uk/13030/1/_lha-011_pers-F_00046E94_ My%20Documents_In%20Dahomey_In%20 Dahomey%20prepublication%20copy.pdf

Seroff, Doug and Abbott, Lynn, *Ragged but Right: Black Traveling Shows, 'Coon Songs', and the Dark Pathway to Blues and Jazz*, Jackson: University Press of Mississippi, 2007.

Shaw, Dave, *Casino*, London: Bee Cool Publishing, 2003.

Shaw, Lisa, *The Social History of the Brazilian Samba*, London: Routledge, 2018 (first published by Ashgate Publishing, 1999).

Silvester, Victor, *Modern Ballroom Dancing*, London: Random House, 2005 (originally published 1927).

Stearns, Marshall and Stearns, Jean, *Jazz Dance: The Story of American Vernacular Dance*, Boston: Da Capo Press, 2nd revised edition, 1994.

Stevens, Tamara and Stevens, Erin, *Swing Dancing (The American Dance Floor)*, Santa Barbara: Greenwood, 2011.

Sublette, Ned, *The World That Made New Orleans: From Spanish Silver to Congo Square*, Chicago: Lawrence Hill Books, 2008.

Thompson, Ahmir Questlove, *Soul Train: The Music, Dance, and Style of a Generation*, New York: Harper Design, 2013.

Thompson, Katrina Dyonne, *Ring Shout, Wheel About: The Racial Politics of Music and Dance in North American Slavery*, Urbana: University of Illinois Press, 2014.

Thompson, Robert Farris, *Tango: The Art History of Love*, New York: Pantheon Books, 2005.

Tucker, Sherrie, *Dance Floor Democracy: The Social Geography of Memory at the Hollywood Canteen*, Durham: Duke University Press, 2014.

Turner, David, *A Passion for Tango: A Thoughtful, Provocative and Useful Guide to That Universal Body Language, Argentine Tango*, Dingley: Dingley Press, 2004.

Vianna, Hermano, edited and translated by John Charles Chasteen, *The Mystery of Samba: Popular Music & National Identity in Brazil*, Chapel Hill: University of North Carolina Press, 1999.

Wallace, Carol McD., et al., *Dance: A Very Social History*, New York: Rizzoli, 1986.

Walkowitz, Daniel J., *City Folk: English Country Dance and the Politics of the Folk in Modern America*, New York: New York University Press, 2010.

Winstanley, Russ, *Soul Survivors: The Wigan Casino Story*, revised edition, London: Robson Books, 2003.

PICTURE CREDITS

All images from the collections of the British Library except the following:

7 Photo by Dave J. Hogan/Getty Images; **8, 29a, 30, 33al, 33ar, 50, 55, 56, 65, 107, 113, 114, 133, 134** New York Public Library; **36, 37, 41, 46, 54, 57, 58, 68, 71, 79, 82, 90–91, 92, 93, 97, 98, 128–129, 149** Library of Congress; **63** LACMA, Gift of Gregory Peck; **64** Archivio General de la Nación, Argentina; **73** Mary Evans Picture Library; **89, 99, 100–101, 102, 104, 142–143, 160, 166, 176** Private Collection; **103** University of Miami Library, Cuban Heritage Collection; **106** Michel Serraillier/Gamma-Rapho/Getty Images; **108** Jean Manzon/AFP/Getty Images; **109** Celso Pupo/Shutterstock; **112** Beinecke Rare Book and Manuscript Library, Yale University; **125** Bibliothèque Marguerite Durand, Paris; **136** Raymond H. Fogler Library, University of Maine; **137** Archive Photos/Getty Images; **139** Photo by Maurice Seymour/Michael Ochs Archives/Getty Images; **140** Photo by Weegee(Arthur Fellig)/International Center of Photography/Getty Images; **141** Photo by Mario De Biasi/Mondadori/Getty Images; **159** Photo by Felix Man/Picture Post/Hulton Archive/Getty Images; **165** Photo by Kurt Hutton/Picture Post/Hulton Archive/Getty Images; **174, 184** LMPC/Getty Images; **175** Photo by Joseph McKeown/Picture Post/Hulton Archive/Getty Images; **183** Photo by David Redfern/Redferns/Getty Images; **186–187** Photo Jean-Paul Goude; **189** Photo Peter Williams; **190** Freestyle Records; **192** Photo by Rita Barros/Getty Images; **195, 196** Photo by Linda Vartoogian/Getty Images.

NOTES

01. EUROPEAN MELODIES

1   John Playford, *The English Dancing Master: or, plaine and easie rules for the dancing of country dances, with the tune to each dance*, Binstead: Dance Books, 2013 (originally published 1623–86?).

2   S. Foster Damon, *The History of Square-Dancing*, Barre: Massachusetts, 1957, p.8.

3   Daniel J. Walkowitz, *City Folk: English Country Dance and the Politics of the Folk in Modern America*, New York: New York University Press, 2010, p.77.

4   Molly Engelhardt, *Dancing Out of Line: Ballrooms, Ballets, and Mobility in Victorian Fiction and Culture*, Athens: Ohio University Press, 2009, p.36.

5   Skiles Howard, *The Politics of Courtly Dancing in Early Modern England*, Amherst: University of Massachusetts Press, 1998, pp.1–25.

6   Dave Haslam, *Life After Dark: A History of British Nightclubs and Music Venues*, London: Simon & Schuster, 2015, p.12.

7   Engelhardt, *Dancing Out of Line*, pp.1–2.

8   Marion Kant, ed., *The Cambridge Companion to Ballet*, Cambridge: Cambridge University Press, 2007, p.53.

9   Rodreguez King-Dorset, *Black Dance in London, 1730–1850: Innovation, Tradition and Resistance*, Jefferson: McFarland & Company, 2008, p.113.

10   Melinda J. Gough, *Dancing Queen: Marie de Médicis' Ballets at the Court of Henri IV*, Toronto: University of Toronto Press, 2019, p.129.

02. AMERICAN RHYTHMS, AFRICAN BEATS

11   Ned Sublette, *The World That Made New Orleans: From Spanish Silver to Congo Square*, Chicago: Lawrence Hill Books, 2008, pp.187–90.

12   Marshall Stearns and Jean Stearns, *Jazz Dance: The Story of American Vernacular Dance*, Boston: Da Capo Press, 2nd revised edition, 1994, pp.18–24.

13   Ibid., pp.11–17.

14   Ibid., p.176.

15   Lynne Fauley Emery, *Black Dance: From 1619 to Today*, Princeton: Princeton Book Company, 1988, pp.91–2.

16   Stearns, *Jazz Dance*, pp.96–98.

17   Tamara Stevens and Erin Stevens, *Swing Dancing (The American Dance Floor)*, Santa Barbara: Greenwood, 2011.

18   Doug Seroff and Lynn Abbott, *Ragged but Right: Black Traveling Shows, 'Coon Songs', and the Dark Pathway to Blues and Jazz*, Jackson: University Press of Mississippi, 2007, p.62.

19   Theresa Saxon, *In Dahomey in England: A (Negative) Transatlantic Performance Heritage*, University of Central Lancaster, 2015. Available at: http://clok.uclan.ac.uk/13030/1/_lha-011_pers-F_00046E94_My%20Documents_In%20Dahomey_In%20Dahomey%20prepublication%20copy.pdf

20   Katrina Hazzard-Gordon, *Jookin': The Rise of Social Dance Formations in African-American Culture*, Philadephia: Temple University Press, pp.89–90.

21   Seroff and Abbott, *Ragged but Right*, pp.3–8.

22   Daniel James Cole and Nancy Deihl, *The History of Modern Fashion From 1850*, London: Laurence King Publishing, 2015, pp.134–136.

23   Eve Golden, *Vernon and Irene Castle's Ragtime Revolution*, Lexington: University Press of Kentucky, 2007.

24   Ibid., p.86.

25   Ibid., p.196.

03. THE TANGO

26   Robert Farris Thompson, *Tango: The Art History of Love*, New York: Pantheon Books, 2005, p.126.

27   George Reid Andrews, *Afro-Latin America, 1800–2000*, Oxford: Oxford University Press, 2004, p.121.

28   Thompson, *Tango: The Art History of Love*, pp.150–67.

29   Mike Gonzalez and Marianella Yanes, *Tango: Sex and Rhythm of the City*, London: Reaktion Books, 2013, p.42.

30   David Turner, *A Passion for Tango: A Thoughtful, Provocative and Useful Guide to That Universal Body Language, Argentine Tango*, Dingley: Dingley Press, 2004, pp.5–6.

31   Jo Baim, *Tango: Creation of a Cultural Icon*, Bloomington: Indiana University Press, 2007, p.20.

32   Turner, *A Passion for Tango*, p.8.

33   Baim, *Tango: Creation of a Cultural Icon*, p.40.

34   Ian Driver, *A Century of Dance: A Hundred Years of Musical Movement, from Waltz to Hip Hop*, London: Hamlyn, 2000, p.67.

35   Gonzalez and Yanes, *Tango: Sex and Rhythm of the City*, p.22.

36   Kathy Davis, *Dancing Tango: Passionate Encounters in a Globalizing World*, New York: New York University Press, 2015, p.4.

37   Marta E. Savigliano, *Tango and the Political Economy of Passion*, Boulder: Westview Press, 1995, pp.40–8.

38   Baim, *Tango: Creation of a Cultural Icon*, pp.28–31.

39   Davis, *Dancing Tango: Passionate Encounters in a Globalizing World*, pp.127–54.

40 Baim, *Tango: Creation of a Cultural Icon*, p.62.

41 Thompson, *Tango: The Art History of Love*, p.242.

42 Ibid., p.242.

43 James Nott, *Going to the Palais: A Social and Cultural History of Dancing and Dance Halls in Britain, 1918-1960*, Oxford: Oxford University Press, 2015, p.109.

44 Gonzalez and Yanes, *Tango: Sex and Rhythm of the City*, pp.61-4.

45 Turner, *A Passion for Tango*, p.12.

46 Thompson, *Tango: The Art History of Love*, p.13.

47 Davis, *Dancing Tango: Passionate Encounters in a Globalizing World*, p.26.

04. FOXTROTS AND FIERCE COMPETITION

48 Driver, *A Century of Dance*, pp.30-3.

49 Nott, *Going to the Palais*, p.109.

50 Ibid., p.101.

51 Rudolf Laban, *Choreutics*, Binsted: Dance Books, 2011.

52 Victor Silvester, *Modern Ballroom Dancing*, London: Random House, 2005 (originally published 1927).

53 Arthur Murray, *How to Become a Good Dancer*, New York: Arthur Murray School of Dancing, 1923.

54 Arthur Murray, *The Modern Dances*, New York: Arthur Murray School of Dancing, 1924.

55 Walkowitz, *City Folk*, 2010.

56 Horace McCoy, *They Shoot Horses, Don't They?*, London: Serpent's Tail, 2010 (originally written in 1935).

57 Carol J. Martin, *Dance Marathons: Performing American Culture of the 1920s and 1930s*, Jackson: University Press of Mississippi, 1994, p.5.

58 Ibid., p.6.

59 Ibid., p.42.

60 Ibid., pp.80-1.

05. LATIN NIGHTS

61 Yvonne Daniel, *Rumba: Dance and Social Change in Contemporary Cuba Blacks in the Diaspora*, Bloomington: Indiana University Press, 1995, p.30.

62 Andrews, *Afro-Latin America*, p.121.

63 Peter Manuel and Michael Largey, *Caribbean Currents: Caribbean Music from Rumba to Reggae*, Philadelphia: Temple University Press, 2016, pp.29-32.

64 Caroline Joan S. Picart, *From Ballroom to DanceSport: Aesthetics, Athletics, and Body Culture*, Albany: State University of New York Press, 2006, p.98.

65 Lisa Shaw, *The Social History of the Brazilian Samba*, London: Routledge, 2018 (first published by Ashgate Publishing 1999), p.3.

66 Driver, *A Century of Dance*, p.73.

67 Hermano Vianna, edited and translated by John Charles Chasteen, *The Mystery of Samba: Popular Music & National Identity in Brazil*, Chapel Hill: University of North Carolina Press, 1999, pp.27-8.

68 Brenda Dixon Gottschild, *The Black Dancing Body: A Geography From Coon to Cool*, London: Palgrave Macmillan, 2003, p.225.

69 Stearns, *Jazz Dance*, p.13.

70 Andrews, *Afro-Latin America, 1800-2000*, pp.71-2.

06. THE CHARLESTON

71 Stearns, *Jazz Dance*, p.145.

72 Driver, *A Century of Dance*, pp.59-63.

73 Nott, *Going to the Palais*, p.112.

74 Ibid.

75 Silvester, *Modern Ballroom Dancing*.

76 Nott, *Going to the Palais*, p.101.

77 Filmed by British Pathé and available to view on its website: *The Flat Foot Charleston Made Easy* (1927).

78 Santos Casani, *Casani's 'Come and Do the Charleston'*, London: Francis, Day & Hunter, c.1927.

79 Brenda Dixon Gottschild, *Waltzing in the Dark: African American Vaudeville and Race Politics in the Swing Era*, New York: St Martin's Press, 2000, p.138.

80 Peggy Caravantes, *The Many Faces of Josephine Baker: Dancer, Singer, Activist, Spy*, Chicago: Chicago Review Press, 2015, p.22.

81 Ibid., pp.32-4.

82 Anne Anlin Cheng, *Second Skin: Josephine Baker and the Modern Surface*, Oxford: Oxford University Press, 2011, pp.35-48.

07. THE LINDY HOP

83 Stevens, *Swing Dancing*, p.47.

84 Ibid., pp.46-7.

85 Ibid., pp.46-50.

86 Stearns, *Jazz Dance*, pp.315-16.

87 Stevens, *Swing Dancing*, pp.77-9.

88 Both dancers feature in: James Berry, *Spirit Moves: A History of Black Social Dance on Film, 1900-1986. Part 1: Jazz Dance from the Turn of the Century to 1950*, Flemington: Dancetime Publications, 2008 (DVD).

89 Available to view: https://www.youtube.com/watch?v=trsX4GWdc94.

90 Stephen Johnson, *Burnt Cork Traditions and Legacies of Blackface Minstrelsy*, Amherst: University of Massachusetts Press, 2012, pp.73-82.

91 Ibid., pp.77-8.

92 Charles Dickens, *American Notes for General Circulation: Volume 1*, Cambridge: Cambridge University Press, 2009 (originally printed in 1842).

93 Ibid., p.287.

94 Eric Lott, *Love & Theft: Blackface Minstrelsy and the American Working Class*, Oxford: Oxford University Press, 2013, p.118.

95 Gottschild, *Waltzing in the Dark*, p.71.

96 Nott, *Going to the Palais*, p.109.

97 Stevens, *Swing Dancing*, p.111.

98 Ibid., p.68.

99 Norma Miller and Evette Jensen, *Swingin' at the Savoy: The Memoir of a Jazz Dancer*, Philadelphia: Temple University Press, 1996, p.107.

100 Ibid., p.244.

101 Thomas Owens, *Bebop: The Music and Its Players*, Oxford: Oxford University Press, 1995, pp.3–10.

102 Stevens, *Swing Dancing*, pp.112–13.

103 Black Hawk Hancock, *American Allegory: Lindy Hop and the Racial Imagination*, Chicago: University of Chicago Press, 2013.

104 Stevens, *Swing Dancing*, p.96.

105 Ibid., p.96.

106 Ibid., p.158.

107 Ibid., pp.95–7.

108 Ibid., pp.185.

109 Ibid., pp.184–5.

08. DANCE HALLS

110 Walkowitz, *City Folk*, p.xi.

111 Nott, *Going to the Palais*, p.1.

112 Ibid., p.48.

113 Ibid., pp.14–15.

114 Ibid., p.15.

115 Haslam, *Life After Dark*, p.xiv.

116 Nott, *Going to the Palais*, p.15.

117 Ibid., p.16.

118 Hennessy, Kathryn and Fischel, Anna, eds., *Fashion: The Definitive History of Costume and Style*, London: Dorling Kindersley, 2013, pp.270–311.

119 Nott, *Going to the Palais*, p.271.

120 Cole and Deihl, *The History of Modern Fashion From 1850*, p.269.

09. JIVE AND ROCK 'N' ROLL

121 Cole and Deihl, *The History of Modern Fashion From 1850*, pp.193–230.

122 Reid Badger, *A Life in Ragtime: A Biography of James Reese Europe*, Oxford: Oxford University Press, 1995.

123 Available to view: https://www.huntleyarchives.com/preview.asp?image=1083270&itemw=4&itemf=0001&itemstep=1&itemx=1.

124 Available to view: https://www.britishpathe.com/video/jive-dance.

125 Nott, *Going to the Palais*, p.154.

126 Allan Bérubé, *Coming Out Under Fire: The History of Gay Men and Women in World War II*, Chapel Hill: University of North Carolina Press, 2010, pp.98–127.

127 Stevens, *Swing Dancing*, p.96.

128 Hennessy, Kathryn and Fischel, Anna, eds., *Fashion: The Definitive History of Costume and Style*, London: Dorling Kindersley, 2013, pp.129–36.

129 Lisa Jo Sagolla, *Rock 'n' Roll Dances of the 1950s*, Westport: Greenwood, 2011, pp.46–7.

130 Ibid., pp.47–50.

131 Available to view: https://www.youtube.com/watch?v=2-tbu0MJIIQ&t=160s.

132 David Nowell, *The Story of Northern Soul: A Definitive History of the Dance Scene That Refuses to Die*, London: Portico, 2011.

10. DANCE CRAZES AND DANCE-FLOOR COOL

133 Tim Lawrence, *Love Saves the Day: A History of American Dance Music Culture, 1970-1979*, Durham: Duke University Press, 2003, pp.5–32.

134 For further reference watch *Saturday Night Fever - The Ultimate Disco Movie* (2017), a BBC documentary presented by Bruno Tonioli that explores the making of *Saturday Night Fever*. The documentary has a short feature with Deney Terrio teaching John Travolta locking and an interview regarding the movements and their original roots.

135 For further reference see *Rodney P's Jazz Funk* (2020), a BBC Four documentary about Black British music culture and the jazz-funk movement.

136 Mark 'Snowboy' Cotgrove, *From Jazz Funk & Fusion to Acid Jazz: The History of the UK Jazz Dance Scene*, London: Chaser Publications, 2009, pp.254–63.

137 Ibid., pp.265–9.

138 Available to view: https://www.youtube.com/watch?v=GprAj-nr100.

139 Ralph G. Giordano, *Country & Western Dance (The American Dance Floor)*, Santa Barbara: Greenwood, 2011.

140 Rictor Norton, *Mother Clap's Molly House: The Gay Subculture in England, 1700-1830*, London: Gay Men's Press, 1992, p.96.

141 Michael Peppiatt, *Francis Bacon in Your Blood: A Memoir*, London: Bloomsbury Publishing, 2015, pp.49–51.

142 Lawrence, *Love Saves the Day*, p.46.

143 Gottschild, *Waltzing in the Dark*, p.72.

144 Marlon M. Bailey, *Butch Queens Up in Pumps: Gender, Performance, and Ballroom Culture in Detroit*, Ann Arbor: The University of Michigan Press, 2016.

145 Halifu Osumare, *The Africanist Aesthetic in Global Hip-Hop Power Moves*, London: Palgrave Macmillan, 2007, pp.49–60.

146 Jeff Chang, *Can't Stop Won't Stop*, New York: St Martin's Press, 2005, pp.137–40.
DANCING IN TIME · NOTES
205

INDEX

Figures in *italic* refer to pages on which
illustrations appear.